Why Girls' Schools Matter

Why Girls' Schools Matter

Reflections of a Lifelong Advocate

WHITNEY RANSOME

Published by River Grove Books
Austin, TX
www.rivergrovebooks.com

Copyright © 2024 Whitney Ransome

All rights reserved.

Thank you for purchasing an authorized edition of this book and for complying with copyright law. No part of this book may be reproduced, stored in a retrieval system, or transmitted by any means, electronic, mechanical, photocopying, recording, or otherwise, without written permission from the copyright holder.

Distributed by River Grove Books

Design and composition by Irene Chu
Cover design by Irene Chu

Publisher's Cataloging-in-Publication data is available.

Print ISBN: 978-1-63299-945-0

eBook ISBN: 978-1-63299-946-7

First Edition published by Flagship Press
North Andover, MA
https://www.flagshippress.com/

Second Edition

For girls and women everywhere
who continue to seek educational opportunities that bring them
knowledge, joy, security, and fulfillment
—often against great odds.

The world needs you now more than ever.

Fight for the things that you care about,
but do it in a way that will lead others to join you.
—*Supreme Court Justice Ruth Bader Ginsburg*

What you do makes a difference,
and you have to decide what kind of difference
you want to make.
—*Anthropologist Jane Goodall*

TABLE OF CONTENTS

Author's Note *ix*
Introduction *1*

I Becoming a Girls' School Advocate *5*
II Title IX and Its Impact on Girls' Education *11*
III Documenting the Girls' School Advantage *15*
IV The Power of Collaboration *21*
V Organizational Models Ahead of Their Time *25*
VI The Early Years of CGBS *31*
VII The Merger *37*
VIII The Right Place at the Right Time *39*
IX The Importance of Girls' Public Schools *43*
X Crafting the Message *47*
XI Building an Entrepreneurial Enterprise *53*
XII Transitions and Celebrations *59*
XIII Let's Talk About Money *67*
XIV The Global Road *71*
XV A New Decade *75*
XVI Leave Taking *81*
XVII Continuing the Work *85*
XVIII Parting Words *91*

Appendices *93*
Acknowledgments *100*
About the Author *103*

AUTHOR'S NOTE

THE FOLLOWING PAGES are a series of personal memories and reflections based on my 20 years of working with the National Coalition of Girls' Schools (NCGS) as co-founder and co-executive director. To help with this endeavor, I have drawn on the Coalition's archival materials, including timelines, annual reports, photos, correspondence, conference programs, news clippings, NCGS publications, and conversations with early leaders, including my co-founder and co-executive director Meg Moulton.

The book is not intended to be a sequential, comprehensive history of the organization. I will leave that to a future historian. Rather, it is a memoir of my personal journey as it intersected with the challenges, risks, and successes of girls' schools across the nation and around the world.

Memories are, of course, subjective and not always verifiable, so there are bound to be occasional errors in fact. These I acknowledge as of my own making. Yet, I've always believed this is a story that needed to be told, and I have made every effort to tell one part of it as accurately as I can. As was true for my work with NCGS, it has been a labor of love.

Whitney "Whitty" Ransome
April 2024

Introduction

*History is not just a series of dates and events;
it's the story of real people and their impact on the world.*
— COKIE ROBERTS

"Who tells your story?" sings Lin-Manuel Miranda in the finale of his Broadway musical, *Hamilton*. I've been wondering that myself in the years since I left the National Coalition of Girls' Schools (NCGS) in 2008. That is, until now.

Truth be told, *my* story is only part of a much bigger one, the chronicle of a dedicated group effort to raise awareness around the world of the importance of educating girls and women. That is a continuing saga, of course, but the work of NCGS to advance the cause of girls' schools everywhere is a major reason such schools are thriving today.

In an effort to tell that story, I drafted an outline for this book several years ago, wrote a number of chapters, and collected relevant materials. But my efforts stopped in 2018 when my husband, Tom Wilcox, and I retired. I kept thinking I'd get to it someday, once my life became a bit less hectic. But, of course, life's pace is not of one's own making. For many women, the hectic nature of their lives never relents.

At 78 years old, my life continues to be hectic, but in different ways. Yet the phrase "You have to tell your story" has kept rattling around my brain. As confident a woman as I am, I'm also plagued by doubts. Would I remember all the important milestones and details of co-founding and directing NCGS, a portion of my career that spanned 20 years from 1988 to 2008? Who would want to read about my life and work experiences? Would I have the energy and information needed to write a meaningful book? Is it arrogant to think I have something important to say?

Then one day, I was struck by the memory of a book by Anna Fels called *Necessary Dreams: Ambition in Women's Changing Lives* (2005). The author writes that young girls often have images of themselves as astronauts, doctors, authors, environmentalists, and other accomplished professionals. But too often along life's journey, they get derailed by naysayers, bad relationships, illness, and other obstacles that cause them to live with unfulfilled aspirations. Another theme of the book that has remained with me is that women are sometimes reluctant to acknowledge their achievements, to say "I did this, and I'm proud of what I've accomplished." They feel they would be boasting when, in reality, they would be claiming their achievements, as they should.

Even today, women continue to worry about how they're perceived. Jennifer Aniston, actor, producer, entrepreneur, and women's activist, told Ellen Gamerman of *The Wall Street Journal*: "There was a time in my world, my career, where I realized it's not being aggressive or combative or bitchy or emotional to stand up for what you deserve and what you want … [a]nd also be loved and respected. It's hard to achieve" (Aug. 22, 2023).

With some encouragement, I've come to realize that telling the early history of NCGS, and the way my life was both reflected in that work and shaped by it, is something to celebrate and share. But trailblazing was hard work for all of us in those early days, as Aniston stated. I certainly had detours along the way. In what I call my "detour decade" from age 22 to 32, I endured two abusive marriages, lost my mother to suicide, and watched my father remarry four months later. The detours created numerous misgivings.

Perhaps the most disheartening event occurred during my first marriage. Under pressure from my then husband, I dropped out of a PhD program in political science at UNC-Chapel Hill, after being one of only five women accepted. I had to decline an internship, disappointing my undergraduate professor, who had nominated me for the position. For a while, I thought my life had been permanently derailed. But I discovered that there was much more life to live and many more necessary dreams to pursue.

This book is one of those dreams. I hope it will help others—women and men—understand the impact of girls' schools on individuals and on the world. They have certainly had an impact on those of us who've believed in and promoted them through the years. They are a part of my story, just as I am a part of theirs.

Whitney "Whitty" Ransome organizing book materials in her studio office in North Hatley, Canada. Summer 2023.

Why Girls' Schools Matter

–I–
Becoming a Girls' School Advocate

I wouldn't be the person I am today without having gone to a girls' school. I would still be sitting at the back of the class not involved in discussions like I am now.

—RITA, GRADE 12

In *What Now?* by Ann Patchett, the author looks back at her life and recognizes that a cluster of random experiences prepared her for each step in her life and career. So it's been with me. For close to 40 years, I worked in or on behalf of girls' public and private schools, and my career has been fueled by a passionate belief that girls' schools matter. Looking back, I now recognize a series of experiences that helped shape this longstanding commitment to all-girls' education.

Days before my 1963 high school graduation, I sat staring at a pile of neatly wrapped presents on a coffee table in my parents' living room. I suspected that several of the packages contained books whose titles I could only imagine: *What to Know Before Your First Year of College*, *How to Organize Your College Days* or, perhaps, *Be a Team Player in College Sports*. In fact, there were several self-help books along with a charm bracelet, gift certificates, and two savings bonds. But the gift that stood out from the rest was *The Feminine Mystique* by Betty Friedan, published that same year.

My best friend's mother, a woman with a career as a marriage counselor and social worker, gave me that book because she wanted me to realize I had options. Yes, I could be a wife and a mom, but I could also have a profession. *The Feminine Mystique*, with its tattered red book jacket and author's signature scrawled across the title page, sits on my bookshelf all these years later. On page 336 of the chapter "The Forfeited Self," I made a short comment in now-faded blue ink: "Finally she suggests something constructive—a solution to the deathly mystique." The section I'd bracketed reads:

> If women do not put forth, finally, that effort to become all that they have it in them to become, they will forfeit their own humanity. A woman today who has no goal, no purpose, no ambition patterning her days into the future, making her stretch and grow that small score of years in which her body can fill its biological function, is committing a kind of suicide."

Just 30 pages later, my next set of underlining appears: "It took, and still takes, extraordinary strength of purpose for women to pursue their own life plans when society does not expect it of them."

That groundbreaking volume opened my mind to endless personal possibilities and became the first step in a lifetime commitment to ensuring that girls and women everywhere had choices in all aspects of their lives.

My deep belief that girls' schools are a vital part of the national educational landscape also stemmed from my own school experiences. I attended Moorestown Friends School (MFS), a Quaker school in southern New Jersey, where I spent 12 years in an exceptional coed setting. The Friends' values of gender equality, collaborative decision-making, and the good within every person threaded the fabric of the school's culture and climate. Girls and boys enjoyed the same opportunities in every arena, including team sports. I excelled in this environment, earning varsity letters in field hockey, basketball, and my favorite, lacrosse. Participating in sports taught me about teamwork, collaboration, cooperation, leadership, and hard work. Everyone played an essential role.

Although MFS was a coed school, I never had a sense that I was anything but an equal participant in all things. The inherent Quaker values of equality for all created an expectation that life after MFS would be similar. Of course, it was not. But my memories of what life *could* be stayed with me and contributed to my becoming a girls' school advocate.

For that reason, I was deeply honored in 2008 to receive the school's Alice Paul Merit Award, named for one of the most ardent women's rights activists of the early 20th century and given to "an individual who best exemplifies the best qualities of MFS, including honesty, integrity, fairness, a commitment to serve others, and a dedication to equality and justice."

When choosing a college, I gave little thought to whether to attend a coed or all-female school. I chose the Woman's College (WC) of the University of North Carolina, located in Greensboro, for other reasons. Having grown up in New Jersey and attended a small independent school, I wanted to try a different part of the country and a large public college. But at WC, I was able to experience first hand the benefits of a single-sex learning environment, and those benefits were formative.

In high school, I feared math and struggled to get Cs. I rarely raised my hand, believed boys always knew the answers, and concluded I didn't have the mind for mathematical problems. But when I took Algebra II in college with other women sharing the classroom, I asked more questions, took risks with my answers, and learned from a teacher who expected the best from us and assumed we could "get it." I completed the course with an A-. The "can-do" culture within that single-sex classroom created a new level of math confidence in me. In my sophomore year, the Woman's College became the coed University of North Carolina at Greensboro, and so was no longer a female-only institution. But that early exposure stayed with me, as did the women professors and mentors whose presence remained formative.

After college, I taught English as a Second Language in a junior college and in a public high school before joining the faculty as dean of students of an all-boys independent school in Miami in 1974. Halfway through my first year, the school merged with a nearby girls' school. Combining resources, faculties, and campuses seemed like a sound idea to the leadership of the respective schools, particularly as more and more schools and colleges became coed. Based on my Quaker school experience, I envisioned a merger with shared leadership, equal numbers of men and women as department chairs, women in high-level positions, and just as many girls' teams as boys' teams. I had that wrong. The new configuration felt more like a takeover than a merger. None of my expectations were realized.

Perhaps I should have known this would happen. When I joined the boys' school faculty the school newspaper read: "Tex Warrington retires as Dean of Students. Our 6'3" football coach will be replaced by Whitney Garner [my married name at the time] a 5'3" attractive young woman from a local public school. Good luck with all our boys, Ms. Garner!!" Still a bit naïve at 29, I wasn't insulted by this description. And when three male coaches strolled into my office, sat across from me, and propped their feet on my desk, a power play went into motion, one that would reappear in other ways. Students in my 9th-grade Ancient History class pushed their textbooks to the floor, a defiant student in another class ignored the dress code daily, and an 11th-grade student was absent 40 days with no consequences. I was being tested.

Ultimately, I told the coaches to remove their feet from my desk, gave the book-dropping students extra homework, expelled the boy ignoring the dress code, and called the parents of the truant 11th-grader. Over time, I learned to stand my ground.

When the girls' and boys' schools came together in a new configuration, the only female who retained her original administrative position was the boys' school librarian. All the prime leadership positions were held by males. All too often, I'd hear the boys say of the girls, "Man, is she a hot one," rather than, "She had a good point in our chemistry class."

Not long after the merger, Jill Kerr Conway, president of Smith College, a female-only institution, came to campus and spoke to alumnae of the area's girls' schools. Her comments addressed the many benefits of an all-women's college culture, among them equal opportunity for all to be leaders in every area of college life, high expectations in all disciplines, a safe and encouraging environment for taking risks, and inspiring role models. For the first time, she gave words to the kind of experience I'd been seeking since I left Moorestown Friends School and the Woman's College of UNC. Standing in a crowd of other women, my view of why girls' and women's institutions mattered firmly took hold.

My passion about women's issues intensified during this decade as a result of my lobbying for passage of the Equal Rights Amendment (ERA) in Florida. I was honored to meet Betty Friedan during that period when she came to Florida to support the efforts of thousands of like-minded women. I took pride in being one of them. "Equality of rights under the law shall not be denied or abridged by the United States or by any State on account of sex." These few words argued for the equal application of the U.S. Constitution to both females and males. The ERA was introduced into every session of Congress between 1923 and 1972, the year it finally passed, and the amendment was sent to the states for ratification. When the deadline of June 1982 arrived, the ERA had been ratified by 35 states, leaving it three states short of the 38 required. As an ERA coordinator for Common Cause, I wrote pamphlets, gave speeches, made media appearances across the state, and debated opponents, including the staunch and vocal antifeminist Phyllis Schlafly. But in the end, Florida voted against the ERA. This frustrating defeat after all the hard work was deflating, but I chose to take it as a challenge and became even more determined to advocate for women.

By the late 1970s, I had left Miami and begun work as director of admissions and financial aid at Dana Hall School, an independent all-girls' day and boarding school in Wellesley, Massachusetts. At Dana Hall, I saw first hand just how transformative the single-sex educational experience could be for adolescent girls. Students were confident, not afraid of taking academic risks or expressing their opinions. They were leaders, knew that failures were part of learning, worked collaboratively, and learned that teamwork brought the best results. I saw growth patterns among the Dana girls that were countercultural at a time when the messages of the so-called real world did not serve them well. These girls cared more about what they were thinking than what they were wearing. They seemed comfortable in their own skin regardless of body type. They behaved in age-appropriate ways and didn't assume older personae as the media would have them do. And they could be smart and proud of it.

Six years after my Dana admissions days, I was asked by a group of prominent girls' school leaders to help address the threat of declining enrollment among girls' schools. They told me they had sought me out because I had reversed a downward enrollment trend at Dana, started my own marketing and admissions consulting business, helped several schools develop comprehensive recruiting programs, and become a media spokeswoman on girls' issues. "We need someone to assist us in reversing the effect of outdated perceptions about our schools," they said. "We can't keep losing students and survive."

I knew they were right and was excited by the prospect of being part of the solution. "Yes!" I answered without hesitation. "I'm in."

–II–
Title IX and Its Impact on Girls' Education

When I graduated from my girls' school,
I felt like I could take on the world.

—KATE, GRADUATE

"Athletic competition builds character in our boys. We do not need that kind of character in our girls, the women of tomorrow," wrote Connecticut Superior Court Justice John Clark FitzGerald in 1971. Judge FitzGerald issued his statement when dismissing a lawsuit filed on behalf of female athletes in the state of Connecticut who wanted to participate in non-contact sports on boys' teams. It is impossible to consider the importance of education for girls and women without talking about the judge's oft-cited comment and the transformational events that followed it. Although he thought girls need not participate in sports, a bill enacted in 1972, commonly called Title IX, changed the cultural landscape for girls and women throughout the United States and contradicted his restrictive judgment.

The preamble to "Title IX of the Educational Amendment to the Civil Rights Act" reads, in part:

> No person in the United States shall, on the basis of sex, be excluded from participation in, be denied the benefits of, or be subject to discrimination under any educational programs or activity receiving federal financial assistance.

Top: Photo by Warren K. Leffler, 1970
Women carrying banners and signs while marching down a street in Washington, D.C., during a demonstration in favor of equal rights for women.

Bottom: U.S. Senator Birch Bayh jogs with Purdue students in the 1970s. Title IX, which Bayh crafted and President Richard Nixon signed into law on June 23, 1972, helped give thousands of women and girls access to competitive sports. [Photo courtesy of the Birch Bayh Photo Collection of the Indiana University Libraries]

That simple statement opened doors in the many educational areas where females had been largely unwelcome.

During the decades prior to Title IX, countless girls and women faced discrimination, racism, homophobia, prejudice, and ridicule in their athletic pursuits. Women were warned that competitive athleticism was not only unfeminine but also proof of lesbianism. Female athletes in team sports were often depicted as physically unattractive, and women were told that such physical exertion would hurt their reproductive organs and even their marriage prospects. Marginalized and trivialized, girls' teams had to raise their own money through bake sales or car washes, make their own uniforms, or wear their school gym suits—never a favorite option. Girls' teams often played in near-empty gymnasiums. Cheerleaders received much more attention than female team members, but not for their athletic feats, which were nonetheless impressive.

When Title IX is mentioned, even today more than 50 years after its passage, many people believe it relates only to athletics. But though it is responsible for the steady advances in women's sports at every level, athletics were just one of numerous key areas addressed by the law. As all-male educational institutions began to open their doors to women in the 1970s, Title IX ensured equal access under the law to all the programs that were open to males.

By the start of the 1980s, Title IX had engendered a broad-based commitment to educational equity. But it is also true that the fervor of that era led many to question the relevance and efficacy of girls' schools. Did they still make a difference? After all, girls' schools historically existed to provide quality education for young women denied access to formerly all-male schools. Single-sex education began to be seen by some as anachronistic, out of touch with the "real world," and no longer relevant. As a result, enrollment in all-girls' schools plummeted during this decade.

But "the real world" turned out to less equitable than many had assumed following the enactment of Title IX, and a handful of girls' school leaders became deeply troubled by the assumptions and misperceptions about schools devoted to the education of girls and women. Rachel Belash, head of Miss Porter's School in Connecticut, and Arlene Gibson, head of Kent Place School in New Jersey, issued calls to action among their girls' school colleagues.

These visionary women had no doubt about the value and benefits of single-sex education, and their goal was to document those benefits and share that information broadly. Based on my own school experiences and my work at the all-girls' Dana Hall School in Massachusetts, I was eager to join their efforts and help enlist the support of others.

At the time, a great deal of transformative work was being done in educational theory, cognitive development, and gender studies, and those important contributions validated our belief that girls' schools were an essential part of the educational landscape. We realized that to survive we needed to document the girls' school advantage in a compelling way and demonstrate the value, benefits, and positive outcomes of studying in an all-girls' environment. Title IX was indeed a huge step forward. But it would take a consolidated effort—the kind of teamwork women were now able to engage in publicly and with confidence—to bring about the renaissance in girls' and women's schools that would take place in the coming decades.

— III —
Documenting the Girls' School Advantage

*At a girls' school, you can be who you are.
You can say what you think and feel, and that's what
prepares you for the real world.*

—ALEX, GRADE 11

In 1981 my husband, Tom Wilcox, became headmaster of Concord Academy (CA), an independent, coeducational boarding and day school, serving grades 9–12 on a bucolic 39-acre campus in the historic town of Concord, Massachusetts. With this appointment, we began a new chapter in our lives, which brought significant changes for us both.

After our first year, I knew the extensive travel, daily commuting, and demanding work of my job as director of admissions and financial aid at Dana Hall School in Wellesley, Massachusetts, would keep me from sorting out my life as a headmaster's wife. There was no roadmap for the role I might play at CA. I'd observed how many other spouses had defined their lives. The traditional role of a female spouse of a headmaster at that time was behind the scenes and primarily social. I wasn't sure I wanted to go down that path. At the same time, Tom and I were trying to start a family. After three miscarriages, adoption was the path we chose. I needed time and space to reimagine what a career, motherhood, and

Why Girls' Schools Matter

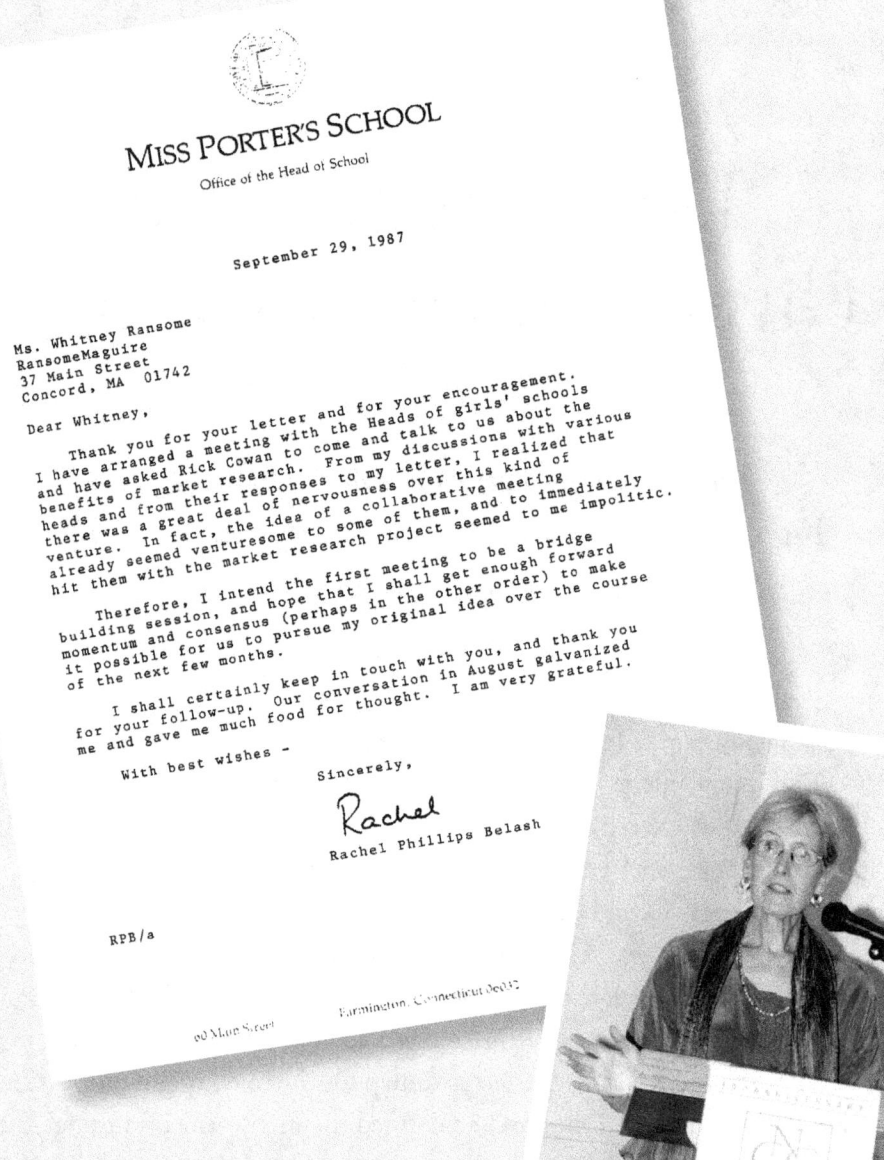

Letter from Rachel Belash, head of Miss Porter's School, thanking Whitney Ransome for encouraging her to urge other girls' school heads to pursue market research, and Rachel Belash speaking at the 10th anniversary celebration of NCGS.

supporting Tom's work might look like, so I had important choices to make.

With all that in mind, I decided to leave my position at Dana Hall in 1982. But I knew I would miss being actively engaged in my own work, so after conversations with Tom, I started a private-school consulting business based out of a second-floor bedroom of the head's house at 228 Main Street in Concord. During my eight years in the admissions field, three at Ransom-Everglades School in Miami, Florida, and five at Dana Hall, I'd developed a broad knowledge about the best ways to attract families to a particular type of school. At Dana, I led the school to its highest enrollment in 10 years, drawing on public relations, branding, financial aid, marketing, qualitative research, and retention strategies to achieve that success. This multifaceted approach to filling a school became known as "enrollment management." I embraced such a methodology in my consulting work and began promoting my services to private schools around the country.

While I had the necessary experience with most of the enrollment management strategies, I lacked a hands-on *quantitative* market research background. I understood the value of gathering qualitative information—through personal interviews, stories, opinions—but the type of research that sought quantifiable data and utilized statistical analysis eluded me. Using calculation tools to measure people's school choice processes, their educational values, and how they viewed one school versus another required skills I didn't possess. The label "math whiz" never appeared next to my name. Many say that such work is both art and science. I could handle the art side but needed to add the science.

To help fill this gap in my knowledge, I joined the firm Enrollment Management Consultants (EMC) and a research team led by the firm's president, Jack Maguire, former dean of enrollment management at Boston College. I brought to the firm an extensive knowledge of private elementary and secondary-school education, a business niche EMC had explored but not mastered. In several instances, I had secured independent school clients that EMC had also pursued. After three interviews and exploratory discussions, I helped establish an independent school division of EMC called Ransome/Maguire. This partnership set the stage for a major shift in my career.

In August 1987, while working at EMC, I received a call from school head Rachel Belash, who knew that girls' boarding schools faced a significant enrollment threat since the decision by many prominent all-boys' schools to open their doors to girls. She believed some kind of market research project was needed and asked how I might go about such a project, what it might cost, how it would be executed, and what I would suggest as next steps.

Rachel had written to other boarding school heads about a collaborative marketing project urging them to join with her to underwrite the cost. Later that fall, a group of interested school heads joined her in a meeting. Also present was Rick Cowan, director of the Boarding Schools Program at the National Association of Independent Schools (NAIS), begun by Tom Wilcox some years earlier and now known as The Association of Boarding Schools (TABS). Rick was called in by Rachel because he had an overall picture of the health of boarding schools nationally.

The assembled group discussed the possible benefits of joint market research. By December, a steering committee had been formed, and in January 1988, the group agreed to interview five consulting firms. EMC was one of the five, and ultimately secured the contract and was asked to direct the project at a cost of $39,000. By February, 39 girls' boarding schools received an invitation to join at $400 each. Twenty-six answered the call with no clear view of what the outcomes might be.

The girls' school educators whom Rachel gathered held the firm belief that their schools had successfully served students of many abilities and backgrounds for generations. What was common among these schools was a longstanding commitment to learning environments that placed girls first and foremost. What set them apart from other schools was an in-depth understanding of how girls learn and succeed. Their understanding came from years of observation, comments by teachers about the ways girls learn best, informal surveys, and testimonials by students and alumnae.

Girls' school leaders were equally informed by the groundbreaking work of Carol Gilligan. In her 1982 book, *In A Different Voice: Psychological Theory and Women's Development*, Gilligan asserted that women and men speak in a different way when they confront ethical dilemmas. Her concepts fostered a new commitment to observing classroom behavior in coed and all-girls' schools. It became clear through this observation that girls were often held back from full participation and achievement in coed classrooms, where boys tended to dominate and attract more attention from teachers. Over the next decade, numerous groups would add their own research-based assessments that demonstrated how girls were being shortchanged in coed settings.

In the minds of girls' school advocates, all-girls' environments offered not only "equal opportunity but every opportunity," a phrase coined by Nannerl O. Keohane, then president of Wellesley College. At girls' schools, all the speakers, leaders, players, writers, singers, and athletes were girls. Female mentors and role models were abundant. The competitive, chilly classroom climate that sometimes permeated coeducational institutions was replaced by a more collaborative model, and female students were not treated like second-class citizens.

One of the many things that surprised us at the time was that the decision by former boys' and men's educational institutions to accept girls and women was not accompanied by studies that documented how a coed environment would serve female students. That was an important oversight, and we did not want to make the same mistake. Rachel Belash's group shared a deep understanding of the girls' school advantage through their many years of experience and observations. But they knew these qualitative opinions would be strengthened by quantitative analysis. Sure enough, in 1988, in nearly 700 phone interviews with families across the country conducted by the EMC research team, girls' schools were cited for their academic excellence and their ability to provide a communal environment that encouraged personal and academic exploration in a supportive culture. Single-sex schools were seen as ideal settings for adolescent girls, since they supported appropriate risk-taking, encouraged academic excellence, prepared girls for college and the real world, and fostered a sense of leadership and self-development.

The findings in our research report filled hundreds of pages. I was not involved in the writing of the technical, quantitative aspects of the surveys; I left that to the actual research team at EMC. My job was to plot next steps based on the vast volume of collected data. I did that in a final chapter, entitled "The Role of the Coalition." Today, tucked in a storage bin of my personal archives is the rough draft of this chapter printed out on spooled printer paper with penciled-in edits. Little did I know then that my thoughts would be adopted, and a slow-moving but powerful revolution in girls' schools would begin.

The Girls' School *Difference*

Research conducted and supported by NCGS uncovered several distinguishing qualities of all-girls' schools:

- They create risk-taking environments designed to teach girls that, in the words of James Joyce, "mistakes are the portals of discovery."

- They counter mass-media influences on female students by giving girls strengthening havens where they can effectively navigate the troubling image of girls in today's media with balance and self-assurance.

- They support a can-do philosophy. All leaders, movers, and doers are female. Girls' schools show their students that a girl can be president, a girl can play the drums, a girl can take apart and reassemble a bike.

- They ensure that learning takes center stage without social distractions. Without the presence of boys, girls tend to display their intelligence and curiosity more freely.

- They incorporate research indicating that team problem-solving works well for girls by providing opportunities for collaborative learning.

- They guarantee that math, science, and technology are integral curricular components in which girls are expected to participate fully.

- They focus on real-life issues like careers, work life, and money matters, tools young women need to be self-sufficient.

- They nurture a culture of caring, collaboration, healthy competition, and mutual support that honors women's voices and values their perspective.

- They promote athletics as a way for girls to learn the benefits of being part of a team and to develop leadership, individual talent, physical strength, resilience, a sense of competence, and the ability to win and lose with grace.

This list, in slightly different form, first appeared in *The Fordham Law Journal*, Vol. 29, (2001) in an article entitled "Why Girls' Schools? The Difference in Girl-Centered Education," by Whitney Ransome and Meg Milne Moulton. Available at: https://ir.lawnet.fordham.edu/ulj/vol29/iss2/5

–IV–
The Power of Collaboration

Each girl comes with their own experience, but when we come together it's like a family.

—BRIELLE, GRADE 6

I first met Meg M. Moulton when I joined Enrollment Management Consultants (EMC) in 1986. At EMC, she worked as a principal consultant within the college admissions field, having been an admissions counselor at Wheaton College, her alma mater, in Norton, Massachusetts, and Simmons College in Boston. EMC had a solid record and reputation for doing market research for colleges and universities that sought to strengthen their student enrollment numbers. Meg's involvement with Ransome/Maguire Associates, a division of EMC with a focus on the independent school market, and her participation in the girls' boarding school research project with me, increased her knowledge of and interest in girls' elementary- and secondary-school education. She soon became a fellow advocate in the effort to identify and promote the advantages of all-girls' schools.

Meg Moulton (left) and Whitty Ransome, NCGS executive directors, at a 1992 meeting in NYC.

In January 1989, Meg, Laura Gaudet, an EMC researcher, and I presented the preliminary findings from the EMC market research project to a newly formed steering committee of girls' boarding school heads. Also in the group were two girls' school admissions directors recently added to the committee: Olive Long of Dana Hall, and Nancy Betts Hays of Garrison Forest School. In light of her history as a leader among admissions directors, Olive soon became co-chair of the steering committee with Rachel Belash.

Among the key findings we presented to the committee was the overwhelming consensus among parents interviewed in the study that girls' schools offered academic strength in a safe, supportive environment that encouraged personal and academic exploration. Girls' schools were seen as ideal settings for adolescent girls since they fostered a culture of educational risk-taking, encouraged and expected academic excellence, promoted leadership and self-advocacy, and prepared girls for college and the real world.

It soon became clear that our report had helped convince the gathered girls' boarding school administrators that there is power in partnership. In the fall of 1989, Meg and I were asked to serve as co-executive directors of a fledging group that came to be known as the Coalition of Girls' Boarding Schools (CGBS). Our mission was to carry out the recommendations I had written in our research project's chapter titled "The Role of the Coalition," which became the template for how the new group would be formed.

Later that year, a group of girls' day school administrators met to discuss organizing their own research project. Following that discussion, girls' day school head Arlene Gibson (Kent Place School) wrote to the day school group, eventually called the Coalition of Girls' Day Schools (CGDS), suggesting they hire the research firm Yankelovich, Clancy, and Shulman, along with public relations consultants Howard Rubenstein Associates. Unlike the EMC-Ransome/Maguire boarding school project, which focused on data collected from parents, the so-called Shulman Study centered on interviews with girls' day school alumnae. Respondents from this second study reported that their girls' school experience had boosted their self-confidence and convinced them that women could accomplish anything. In addition, attending a girls' school had helped them focus on academics and encouraged them to test their intellectual limits without the burden of social constraints.

Using results from their respective research projects, the boarding school and day school coalitions set out to put their research findings to work. For a few years, they did this as parallel groups. Then, between 1990 and 1991, conversations began about a possible merger.

Left: Meg Moulton and Whitty Ransome in San Francisco for a regional member gathering

Below: Meg and Whitty featured in NCGS's 10th Anniversary publication.

Why Girls' Schools Matter

Right (left to right): Meg Moulton, Administrative Assistant Sue Sauer, and Whitty Ransome in the 228 Main St. office in Concord, Massachusetts

Below (left to right): Meg Moulton, Director of Administrative Services Ann Parke, and Whitty Ransome.

–V–
Organizational Models Ahead of Their Time

*At an all-girls' school I've been empowered
to follow my passions and discover who I want to be.*

—MELODY, GRADE 12

It has always been interesting to me how my personal and professional lives often intersected in ways that I was not fully aware of at the time. Little did I realize when we arrived at Concord Academy (CA), for example, that I would be redefining the role of headmaster's wife. At the same time, my early work with the Coalition of Girls' Boarding Schools involved creating a new model for leading an organization at a distance—and from home.

On the same floor as the home office I'd created in an unused bedroom on the second floor of the headmaster's house were the bedrooms of our children, Kate and Christopher. They were young at the time, and being able to be near them while also working made for a convenient way to balance home and work life.

I arrived at CA using my maiden name, Elizabeth Whitney "Whitty" Ransome. During my previous two marriages, I had taken my husbands' last names. But when I got divorced the second time, I was determined to go back to the name that I had had before my life started unraveling. By doing this, I affirmed who I'd once been. I felt empowered by this simple act. Fortunately, Tom had no problem with my doing this, though it took his mother a long while before she stopped calling me Mrs. Wilcox!

Early on, Tom and I made the decision to open our house to Concord Academy parents, students, alumnae/i, trustees, faculty, staff, and visiting guests. In an average year during our 19-year tenure, we would entertain between 2,000 and 3,000 guests in our home, including repeat visitors. We wanted to create a sense of community, connectedness, and enjoyment among all constituents of the school, and our home became a place where that could happen. Thankfully, others did the cooking and cleaning during our evenings of entertaining, and I loved the fact I could sneak upstairs to read and say goodnight to Kate and Chris. I could even go into my office on the sly and file a document or two. I must confess that sometimes, when the activities downstairs didn't require my full attention, I'd disappear to our bedroom and dive into a book of my own.

I enjoyed the role I came to play at CA. I found the position rather easy, since I had a detailed knowledge of how independent schools worked. I was also happy to discover that as a former girls' school that took the bold move to begin accepting boys in 1971, CA had maintained the inclusive, collaborative, supportive culture that had always defined it and that would continue to distinguish it after it went coed.

In addition, there were numerous unexpected personal benefits, including trips to the many places Tom and I went to represent the school. Besides traveling to cities across the U.S., we visited Jordan, Thailand, Hong Kong, Indonesia, South Korea, Taiwan, London, and Paris to meet with parents and alumnae/i, tell the story of the current school, and make the case for philanthropic support.

I'll never forget our visit to Jakarta, where Tom made a pitch for a $1million gift in support of the renovation of one of the colonial houses that lined Main Street in Concord and served as student residences. Tom's vision included adapting these structures for modern use, and he shared this vision with Mr. Admadjaja while I was chatting with his wife. After receiving from the Admajajas a multicolored batik shirt, typical of Indonesia, Tom ducked into a bathroom to change into it. As he emerged, an exultant grin filled his face, and he whispered to me quietly, "We'll be renovating that house!"

Concord Academy's Head's House at 228 Main St. in Concord, Massachusetts, was home to Tom and Whitty's family and served as NCGS's office for 10 years. [Drawing by Peggy Wright]

On another occasion, we traveled to London for a large reception celebrating CA's recent 75th anniversary. With us was Kitty Ames, a CA alumna, parent, and trustee. She often tells the story of Tom's being called to the phone in the middle of a speech. "So Tom goes off to handle a delicate situation back in Concord, and Whitty steps in to continue making his major points," she tells her listeners. "On Tom's return, she gives the microphone to him, and he wraps up his speech." Thankfully, I knew enough about the school and what Tom intended to say to fill in when needed.

In time, the Board of Trustees asked me to write a description of the different tasks I performed on an annual basis. After reading my write-up, the Board decided I should receive a small stipend and be given the official title of Special Assistant to the Head of School, a step I believe was unheard of at the time.

I especially enjoyed doing things for faculty and students that brought the community closer together. I turned a former pony pasture behind our house into a community garden, I organized wreath-making parties in our basement for the winter holiday season, I hosted seders for our Jewish students and faculty, and I created a New Jersey Club since so many community members (including me) had connections to the Garden State. One day, a student asked me where I was from, and I said New Jersey. "Really? Which exit?" she asked. Forever after, she called me Exit 4!

Among my fondest memories of entertaining were the faculty parties at the end of each semester. At one of these December gatherings, we turned up the music, rolled up the rug in our living room, pushed back the furniture, and danced as if we were teenagers. The group's enthusiasm was such that our family Christmas tree in the corner of the room fell down. Gasps and laughter filled the room. The following year, the maintenance staff devised a way to attach a wire from the tree to the wall so that it would never happen again.

I didn't realize during our 19 years at CA that what I did mattered to people. At the time of our departure in 2000, we were given four CA-green boxes with gold lettering recording the years of our service. Within one of the boxes were countless thank-you notes, cards, and scraps of paper citing how important our work on behalf of multiple constituencies had been.

Just recently after writing former CA colleague Ted Scott who'd just lost his wife, Esther, I received this remarkable reply:

> I've always wanted to tell you a story about Esther that concerns you. When I took the job at CA, it involved a pay cut from what I made as a teacher in a local public school, and it involved my traveling and being away from home when we had a four-year-old and she was undergoing chemotherapy. So there wasn't a lot about my coming to CA that pleased her.
>
> What turned her around and made her a huge fan of Concord Academy was the hospitality that you and Tom extended to all of us. Your holiday parties and end of year ones, and the warmth of the people she started to get to know at them and, not the least, the chance to dance, all won her over completely and against all odds. She was particularly admiring of your graciousness, Whitty, and every time your name has come up in conversation, Esther affirmed her affection and admiration for you.

I wept when I read Ted's note. I felt his loss and was humbled by Esther's memories of our parties and her thoughts about us. I never imagined the ways in which opening up our home to others could change attitudes. I was equally humbled when on our departure from CA the trustees named a recently built space "The Ransome Room." I was especially pleased that the space was meant to be a gathering place for faculty, students, and school events. It was a wonderful acknowledgment of the thousands of folks who flowed through our home in the course of those 19 years.

My experience reimagining the role of a head of school's spouse was a perfect way for me to begin reimagining what my professional life might look like as Tom and I were raising our children. Over time, my home office at Concord Academy became the locale where Meg and I did the majority of our work when we became co-executive directors of the Coalition of Girls' Boarding Schools (CGBS) in the summer of 1989. We lived about five miles apart, and Meg also had set up a home office.

What we didn't know as we set about our work together was that we were creating a new operational model, just as Tom and I had done for CA. Meg and I gradually forged a shared leadership style in what became a "virtual" enterprise that operated on a shoestring. We had no assistant, used an ironing board to organize mailings, and cited my personal phone number as the contact point. Given that dues were low for the original 31 CGBS member schools, an inexpensive operation was not a choice—it was an imperative.

"Nimble, entrepreneurial, Cheap Chicks." These are a few of the terms often used when the Coalition's leaders referred to Meg and me. In our first months as co-executive directors we created a letterhead, a directory of 1989–90 member schools that we photocopied and distributed. And in June 1990, we organized the first CGBS membership meeting at MacDuffie School in Granby, Massachusetts, to which we invited heads of schools and admissions directors. The focus during the gathering was on creating a common approach to promoting the benefits and value of a girls' boarding school. It was a small step, but we were on our way.

Polly Vanasse, a teacher at the Nashoba Brooks School in Concord, Massachusetts, testing a model she built as part of a Design Workshop at a Girls and Technology conference. [Photo by Tim Morse]

–VI–
The Early Years of CGBS: 1989–1991
Conferences, Communication, Connections

When we enter a space where we are minorities in STEM, we have to prove even more than boys that we are capable and that we are confident in what we are doing.

—AMANDA, GRADE 12

Math and science were never my best subjects in high school or in college. My undergraduate major was Political Science and International Studies. Seven years after receiving my B.A., I finished graduate school at the University of Miami with a degree in American Studies.

Coming of age in the 1960s, I had visions of going into politics. In 1966, I spent the summer between my junior and senior years of college as one of 13 students chosen from the consolidated University System of North Carolina to work on Capitol Hill with Congressman Frank Thompson Jr. of New Jersey, my home state. During the following summer, I was offered another internship, this time in the newly formed Department of Community Affairs in New Jersey. Unfortunately, the trauma of an early failed marriage set me off course, derailing my dreams of a life working in public policy.

But a side effect of my change in course was that I found myself using math and science in my future work as a consultant on enrollment management strategies and later as a girls' school advocate. I would also discover that a new generation of girls was being encouraged to engage in STEM (Science, Technology, Engineering, and Mathematics) pursuits in school and careers. In October 2023, I happened to be in Newport, Vermont, 30 minutes from the Canadian cottage where Tom and I spend most of our summers. At the Natural Foods Café where I grabbed lunch, I noticed an abandoned copy of *The Newport Daily Express*, which featured an article entitled "Women Can Do: Largest STEM and Trades Conference for High School Girls." The article described a conference that would welcome 400 girls from across the state to participate in hands-on activities designed to expose them to nontraditional careers for women.

As I read that article, I had a flashback to 1989 and remembered a troubling finding from the Coalition of Girls' Boarding Schools research project. Ann Pollina, then head of Westover School in Middlebury, Connecticut, was astonished to learn that parents of girls in all-girls' schools believed that math and science courses and facilities at coed schools were superior to those their daughters had encountered. Dismayed by those reports, Ann suggested that CGBS demonstrate the strength of girls' schools in these subjects by organizing and sponsoring a series of conferences about girls in math, science, and technology. Pollina and Louise Gould, a mathematics teacher at Ethel Walker School in Simsbury, Connecticut, designed the first four-day conference, *The Girls, Math, and Science Symposium*, held at Wellesley College in June 1991. Among the presenters were many accomplished professional women working in STEM fields. They knew from direct experience that girls tended to learn differently, and with this knowledge in hand, classrooms became places where comments such as "I can't do math" changed to "I love math!"

Meg and I were fully engaged in bringing this inaugural symposium into existence. With Ann's help, we secured funding from the Klingenstein Foundation, which gave us $20,000 for each of two years. Half of the grant was designated for the symposium and the other half for our operating funds.

The teaching strategies that emerged from these symposiums became the

basis of three publications: *Girls, Math, and Science Symposium: The Complete Proceedings*; *The Executive Summary*; and *Task Force Reports*. These publications highlighted lessons learned in all-girls' classrooms and recommended strategies that teachers and researchers agreed made a difference to girls' achievement, not just in the classroom but in other single-sex settings as well. Here are some of the major recommendations for helping girls learn and thrive in STEM pursuits:

- Use relevant real-world applications from girls' lives.
- Draw on vocabulary, metaphors, and examples that girls can identify with.
- Teach in collaborative and cooperative ways.
- Call students by name and wait for them to reply before moving on to the next student.
- Encourage academic risk-taking.
- Explore mistakes and acknowledge their value.
- Teach alternative solutions rather than one single right answer to a given problem.

- Use writing as a means of learning any subject, including mathematics.
- Explain through stories.
- Help students see themselves as sources of knowledge.

As it turns out, these strategies became a template for educators in both coed and all-girls' schools, as researchers began to understand and publicize different learning styles and encourage a greater awareness of how to help all students, boys and girls, reach their learning potential through a broader, more enlightened array of teaching strategies.

It is interesting to look back at the role Meg and I played as fledging executive directors for the CGBS as we approached these early symposiums and other such events. We understood that leaders within member schools—heads, admission directors, public relations staff, and development personnel—were busy fulfilling their professional duties in their respective schools. It was our job to articulate, promote, and market what distinguished these schools within the independent-school realm and do the legwork to help organize the group events they chose to sponsor.

A major goal in those early years involved convening the membership and communicating through newsletters and updated membership lists. We also wrote materials that promoted activities organized by the Steering Committee. Shortly after taking on our roles, we published "Of Statistical Note," "The Coalition Digest," and the "The Coalition Chronicle." The content of these pieces emphasized research findings, news from member schools, summaries of relevant articles, and announcements of upcoming events. School leaders frequently displayed these publications in their admissions, development, or heads' offices.

The ultimate goal in almost everything we did at this time was to create a common language for describing the girls' school experience. In June 1990, for example, 45 participants attended the first CGBS membership meeting at The MacDuffie School in Granby, Massachusetts. Several sessions focused on how to use relatable language to promote the benefits of a girls' boarding school. Drawing on numerous findings from the EMC-Ransome/Maguire research report, we developed a series of message points, such as "Not Equal Opportunity, But *Every* Opportunity," "Expect the Best from a Girl and That's What You'll Get," "Not

Your Grandmothers' Girls' School," "It's What She thinks, Not What She Wears that Matters." We hoped that what were then known as "sound bites" would help get our message across in words that would be catchy as well as meaningful.

Then during the fall of 1990, Meg and I convened what we called the *Girls and Women: Our Common Cause* conversation in New York City. We invited the leaders of Girls Scouts of America; Girls, Inc.; the YWCA; the Ms. Foundation; and the Women's College Coalition. All of us represented organizations that served girls in one way or another. The agenda included discussions of our latest projects, our major organizational achievements, our current challenges, our shareable resources, and our thoughts on how we could work together in our advocacy for girls. We did not arrive at any formal agreement, but this widening of our collaborative efforts served not only to bolster our own organizations' efforts but also to advance the cause of girls' education on a larger scale. Meg and I both valued collaboration, and our commitment to it would soon alter the future of CGBS in positive and lasting ways.

NCGS flyer describing the girls' school experience along with tips and a reading list for parents and teachers.

Why Girls' Schools Matter

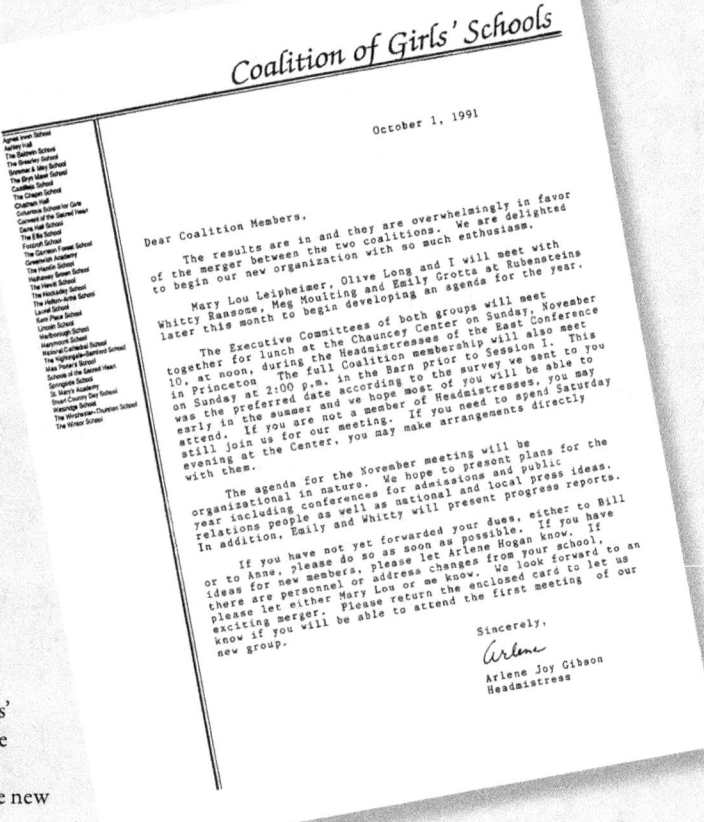

November 1991 letter from Arlene Gibson, head of Kent Place School, announcing to her Coalition of Girls' Day Schools that the group would be merging with the Coalition of Girls' Boarding Schools; and, to its left, the new NCGS logo.

NCGS LISTING OF MEMBER SCHOOLS

Andrews School
Agnes Irwin School
The Annie Wright School
Ashley Hall
Baldwin School
The Brearley School
Brimmer & May School
The Bryn Mawr School
Castilleja School
The Chapin School
Chatham Hall
Columbus School for Girls
Convent of the Sacred Heart
Emma Willard School
Dana Hall School
The Ellis School
The Ethel Walker School
Foxcroft School
The Garrison Forest School

Greenwich Academy
The Grier School
The Hamlin School
Hathaway Brown School
The Hewitt School
The Hockaday School
The Holton-Arms School
Kent Place School
Laurel School
The Madeira School
Marlborough School
Marymount School
The Master's School
Miss Hall's School
Miss Porter's School
National Cathedral School
The Nightingale-Bamford School
Oldfields School
Purnell School

Salem Academy
Schools of the Sacred Heart
Springside School
St Catherine's School
St Margaret's School
St Mary's Academy
St. Scholastica Academy
St Timothy's School
San Domenico School
Santa Catalina chool
Stoneleigh-Burnham School
Stuart Country Day School
Stuart Hall School
Vivian Webb School
Westover School
Westridge School
The Winsor School

November 10, 1991

–VII–
The Merger

*Coalition of Girls' Boarding Schools + Coalition of Girls' Day Schools =
National Coalition of Girls' Schools*

During the summer of 1991, the academic leaders of both the Coalition of Girls' Boarding Schools and the Coalition of Girls' Day Schools held conversations with their respective memberships about the value of merging the two groups. These conversations were driven by a recognition of the common goals and challenges involved in educating girls and by a realization that a merger would lead to more efficient outreach and provide strength in numbers, especially in garnering press attention.

These discussions led participants at the November 1991 meeting of the Headmistresses of the East Conference to agree to form a new organization: the National Coalition of Girls' Schools (NCGS).

Mary Lou Leipheimer of the Foxcroft School in Middleburg, Virginia; Olive Long of Dana Hall School in Wellesley, Massachusetts; and Arlene Gibson of Kent Place School in Summit, New Jersey, formed the new organization's steering committee. Meg and I remained as executive directors of the larger group, and Howard Rubenstein Associates was rehired as our public relations counsel. Fifty-six schools constituted the new membership.

Mary Lou Leipheimer (left), head of Foxcroft School, and Arlene Gibson, head of Kent Place School, helped bring the two coalitions together, along with Olive Long, director of admissions at Dana Hall School.

The strength of the merger derived in large part from the qualities that had distinguished the two original coalitions. The steering committee comprised consummate professionals who had a grasp of both the details and the big picture. As co-directors, Meg and I could bring our managerial skills, research, and school-savvy to carry out their vision. The school administrators could help each other meet their enrollment goals. And we could all be guided and supported by a trusted public relations firm that would bring national visibility to our initiatives.

As co-executive directors of NCGS, Meg and I set about shaping a detailed organizational outline that included governance, administrative structure, membership dues, communication tools, and proposed tasks to be carried out by the two of us and by our public relations counsel. We shared this document with members, accompanied by a letter describing how Meg and I planned to move the new group forward. (See Appendix B, page 97.)

Shortly after the merger, in January 1992, an article entitled "Groups Coalesce to Tout Benefits of Girls' Schools," by Mark Walsh, appeared in *Education Week*. "The all-girls' schools, individually and collectively, have focused their research and marketing on promoting their belief that single-sex education offers girls a better classroom environment, a more inclusive curriculum, and more leadership opportunities," Walsh wrote. "In an upcoming project, the coalition will compare mathematics and science teaching for girls in single-sex versus coed schools."

I am quoted in the article as saying, "We are marketing the concept of single-sex education. But research is the key word for what this organization will stay focused on.... We hope the findings of that research will document what we know intuitively: that girls in girls' schools are taking more math and science courses than those in other schools."

The positive response to this article confirmed our belief that by joining forces, the boarding and day school contingents could increase their influence and strengthen their impact. (See Appendix A, page 95, for a timeline of the merger.)

–VIII–
The Right Place at the Right Time

We're going to school not to meet boys
but to learn about the world as well as ourselves.
—MIAYUNIQUE, GRADE 11

After the boarding and day groups joined to form the National Coalition of Girls' Schools (NCGS), the combined group began a comprehensive campaign to heighten the visibility of the girls' school experience. As co-executive directors, Meg and I had a busy first year, crafting our work from a skeletal job description. At the outset, there were a number of organizational tasks to accomplish. Some of our earliest assignments included establishing a Statement of Purpose, developing membership lists, maintaining enrollment data, connecting with other independent school organizations, providing marketing advice to individual schools, creating a media contact list, and positioning ourselves as thought leaders on nearly any topic connected to the education of girls.

In addition, the five-page 1991–92 Annual Report to the membership listed a diverse array of activities, including soliciting new member schools, serving as experts on girl-related subjects, creating liaisons with other educational and research organizations, and coordinating the publication of three *Girls, Math, and Science* books.

It is hard to remember how Meg and I began dividing up responsibilities. We slipped naturally into a fluid process, jointly writing marketing materials and sharing the establishment of connections to other groups within the U.S. and with girls' school groups in England, Canada, and Australia. Meg took the lead on financials and writing reports, while my attention went to conference planning, production of low-cost or free publications, and outreach to girls' public schools. Our to-do lists became the centerpiece of our many meetings over coffee at a local shop in Concord, where we both lived and maintained home offices. We divvied up the assignments and took great pleasure in returning to our next tête-à-tête with items crossed off our progress reports.

I loved the work. As a start-up group, we had a nimble and entrepreneurial approach to so much of what we did. Plus, we had significant latitude in conceiving new ideas backed by an amazing set of board members, most of them women. Board meetings were stimulating, full of laughter, and imbued with a strong sense that together we could bring girls' schools back from the brink of extinction. We realized that the Coalition's impact on the world of education would benefit from being in the right place at the right time—with the right people.

Within the first few years of NCGS's existence, our work was enhanced by a number of new developments in the field of educational research. In the early 1980s, relatively little was being written with a spotlight on girls. Carol Gilligan's *In A Different Voice*, an important, enlightening study of girls' development, appeared in 1982, but its influence took time to grow. Gradually, other educational studies on different gender-based learning styles appeared, along with reports on the lower number of girls and women in nontraditional career pursuits, the dearth of women's voices in school curriculums, and evidence of variations in both the development and functioning of male and female brains. As the 1980s advanced, important work was being done in these areas at the Center for Research on Women at Wellesley College, pioneered by Peggy McIntosh. The dissemination of the Coalition's research, through publications and media coverage, contributed to this new focus on girls, and we began to see a gradual shift in public attitudes that supported our cause.

During the feminist revolution of the 1970s, talk of innate differences in the behaviors of men and women was considered politically incorrect. Social and cultural origins, rather than genetic origins, were held to explain gender disparities, particularly in professions such as engineering, technology, and architecture. These social and cultural factors were also used to explain the tendencies of boys to be more quantitative and spatially adept. Yet studies of the brain revealed that gender differences are rooted as much in chemistry and structure of the brain as in the manner in which girls and boys are raised. The tendencies of girls to be more contemplative, collaborative, intuitive, and verbal, and of boys to be more physically active, aggressive, and more solitary in their working habits, was seen to be related to brain function and development.

The release of these scientific findings allowed the NCGS research to be seen through a new lens, and the educational debate on gender equity began to evolve. The driving question was no longer limited to whether girls and women had equal access and equal opportunity. New questions were raised about the relative quality of their educational experience and their subsequent outcomes. The ways girls experience school, look at the world, and deal with math, science, and technology do not always mirror the way boys do the same things. This knowledge may seem evident to us today, but at the time it was provocative and carried profound implications. People stopped asking, "What is wrong with the girls? Why aren't they more interested in nontraditional subjects?" Instead, the operative question became, "What is wrong with the way we are teaching and interacting with girls? Why are girls not achieving at levels commensurate with their abilities?"

In the early 1990s, as the NCGS was launching its own research, a slew of reports and books by other groups and individuals gave additional fuel to the debate about the status of girls within the American educational landscape. Two of the most powerful documents came from the American Association of University Women (AAUW). The title of their original findings was "Shortchanging Girls, Shortchanging America," followed soon after by another report called "Growing Smart: What's Working for Girls in Schools."

These reports became the impetus for a nationwide discussion of disparities between girls' and boys' attitudes toward achievement and self-esteem. Boys tended to overestimate their aptitude and skills, while girls tended to understate their abilities. These differences were particularly relevant in the areas of math and science, and they underscored the value of girls learning in a single-sex environment that boosted not only their skills but also their self-confidence.

Throughout the 1990s, bookstores began to feature such influential works as *Failing at Fairness: How American Schools Cheat Girls* (1994) by David and Myra Sadker; *School Girls* (1994) by Peggy Ornstein, named a Notable Book of the Year by *The New York Times*; and "Single-Sex Schooling: Perspectives from Practice and Research" (1999), by the U.S. Department of Education.

Meg and I, along with the Coalition's board members, rejoiced at this new attention on what was and wasn't working for girls. We moved quickly to position ourselves as experts and advocates ready to share the valuable lessons that had already been learned in girls' schools. We believed that girls-only campuses and classrooms represented exciting laboratories for discovery and could serve as an invaluable asset to educators everywhere. At last, the tide had begun to turn in the national debate about why girls' schools matter.

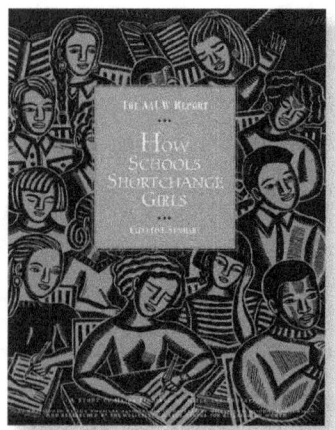

–IX–
The Importance of Girls' Public Schools

*All-girls' schools are great environments to explore
what you're interested in and
in an environment that's safe and supportive.*
—BRIANNA, GRADE 10

Random comments can sometimes change the trajectory of one's life. Soon after graduating from college, I returned to my high school alma mater, Moorestown Friends School in southern New Jersey. As I walked down a familiar hallway, Chester Reagan, a former headmaster of the school, stopped to say hello. As we chatted, he exclaimed out of the blue, "You should teach!" My career aspirations at that point involved getting a job in government or politics, so his comment caught me off guard. Since I lacked a clear path to those professional goals, I gave serious consideration to his suggestion.

Within several months, I started substituting at a local public school in my hometown. Stepping in for an absent teacher has its challenges. I often received lesson plans in subjects I knew nothing about. Frequently, students disrupted my efforts in the classroom by ignoring my questions or talking with each other instead of focusing on the work.

My public school teaching experience changed dramatically when I moved to Puerto Rico with my first husband. I didn't have the qualifications to teach at a local private school, but instead fell into a position at Puerto Rico Junior College, a public institution partly funded by the island government. A new department was under consideration with a focus on English as a Second Language, known familiarly as ESL. My lack of fluency in Spanish turned out to be an asset. That and my youthful enthusiasm. In 1969, ESL curriculum guidelines were nonexistent, and I enjoyed the challenge of helping an emerging group of teachers write lessons plans on a weekly basis.

The students at the junior college had ambitions of their own. Without proficiency in English, however, they were limited in their higher education options. Many of my students had been rejected by the University of Puerto Rico but hoped that improvement in their English language skills might gain them a second chance.

My teaching schedule was part-time, and I walked to my classes on the days I taught. I loved the fact that my students called me "Missy," spoke what is sometimes called Spanglish (an easily understood blend of English and Spanish), and giggled when I mangled my version of their native tongue. Having a flexible work schedule suited me, and I spent my free time learning more about the history, culture, geography, and cuisine of my island home. But the teaching was a highlight, and to this day, I can envision the faces of my students and feel the joy with which they came to school.

After almost three years in Puerto Rico, my husband lost his job there but managed to get another one in Miami in the field of small-airport management. In a dusty file from my early career days, I found a "To Whom It May Concern" recommendation from my ESL department head. She said "Mrs. Garner (my married name at the time) demonstrated initiative, reliability, and industriousness. She was remarkably tactful and cooperative in working with others. And her students expressed their recognition for her willingness to help them and her teaching abilities. We hate to think about losing her. I do believe she can tackle any assignment with more than the average get-up-and-go."

Luckily, ESL teachers were in scarce supply in South Florida. I landed a position at Miami Central High School in the inner city. The student body was a mixture of Latin American immigrants, inner-city African Americans, and low-

The Importance of Girls' Public School

Brochure for the 2009 National Conference on Single-Sex Schools and a letter to Whitney Ransome from Maureen Grogan, director of the Public Schools Conference, offering thanks for NCGS's sponsorship of the program.

income whites. Classes began at 7 a.m., and I taught straight through until noon. It was hard work, but I thrived in this environment and became an advisor to several student government groups.

These experiences during a formative time in my life opened my eyes to the importance of quality education in the public sphere. So many of my students held down part-time jobs to help with family expenses. For them, a high school diploma could make a difference in their career possibilities. I was especially interested in the educational and cultural challenges faced by my female students. Although all my classes were coed, I came to my later work at the National Coalition of Girls' Schools (NCGS) concerned that girls in economically challenged communities were being underserved and too often left out of chances for a better life.

The enactment of Title IX in 1972 prohibited schools that received federal funding from discriminating against students on the basis of sex. The reasoning was partially based on evidence that all-boys' public schools were better equipped and staffed than all-girls' schools. By the mid-1990s, only two all-girls' public schools remained: the Philadelphia High School for Girls and Western High School in Baltimore. According to Ilana DeBare in *Where Girls Come First*, these two schools "did everything they could to keep a low profile and, to their relief, no boys actually tried to test the law."

For all their good intentions, Title IX advocates could not have anticipated the informed analysis of the positive role of girls' schools, which soon resulted in an increase in private girls' school enrollments. In the fall of 1997, NCGS reported that enrollments were up 11.6 % over their 1991 level, and the percentage of member schools at full enrollment had more than doubled (from 24% to 50%) since the 1995–96 school year.

This growing appreciation of girls' schools eventually spilled back into the public sector. DeBare explains in her book that because Title IX did not explicitly prohibit single-sex schools, they were found to be permissible "if there were comparable facilities and services available to the excluded gender." Since 1995, there has been a resurgence of all-girls' public schools throughout the U.S., and they now number more than 200.

Early on in my work with NCGS, I paid visits to the two public girls' schools still open at the time and, with board approval, welcomed them into NCGS membership at no cost. NCGS offered support to these established schools and to the fledging schools that began to spring up over time by sharing our research, publications, and media connections. Plus, we cultivated a relationship with Maureen Grogan, who served as our counterpart at the New York City-based Young Women's Leadership School Network. Maureen and I committed to building connections between our groups, knowing that together we could bring added attention to the importance of single-sex schools.

In 2001, another set of laws helped shift the public school landscape. The U.S. Senate passed an education bill called No Child Left Behind. It included a provision proposed by Sen. Kay Bailey Hutchison (R-Texas) making single-sex education more available in public schools including single-sex classes. She was joined by four other senators: Hillary Clinton (D-New York), Carol Mosley Braun (D-Illinois), Barbara Boxer (D-California), and Barbara Mikulski (D-Maryland). Meg and I met with the legislative coordinators for each of these senators, providing data-driven information about the benefits and outcomes of gender-based learning environments. Twenty-five NCGS heads of school signed a letter endorsing the proposed legislation.

By this time, we at NCGS were beginning to see the positive effects of our work as a coalition. It was exciting to witness that our willingness to welcome all-girls' public schools into our widening partnership was resulting in increased possibilities for underserved populations throughout the country.

– X –

Crafting the Message: Working the Media

*I didn't know I could be a leader
or an advocate for things that I am passionate about.*

—MAYA, GRADE 12

A director of admissions needs strong public speaking skills. Luckily, I had held leadership positions in high school and college, where I frequently stood before an audience to make presentations. As a result, I developed a level of comfort with sharing points of view, suggesting new ideas, and laying out plans of action. We aren't usually aware as young women that every job we take on early in our lives can provide us with valuable skills for future pursuits. These skills became an important segment of my work for NCGS.

Guided first by the public relations firm of Howard Rubenstein, Meg and I fostered relationships with print, TV, and radio contacts, providing content about math and science for girls, gender inequity in coed classrooms, the importance of mentoring, the benefits and outcomes of all-girls' schools, and findings from our ongoing research.

We also offered ourselves as advisors on girl-related topics and were asked to speak to educational groups and organizations around the country. We kept track of relevant news clips from CNN's *Headline News*, NBC's *Dateline*, and ABC's *20/20*, and in 1993 we produced a video of these television segments, which validated our own findings. These third-party stories gave added weight to our proposition that girl-centered schools and activities provided young women with opportunities not easily found elsewhere.

In 1992, we received an invitation to serve on the Ms. Foundation for Women's Advisory Board. We offered our research-based counsel to the group, including supporting the foundation's Take Our Daughters to Work Day and other initiatives. More than half our member schools participated in the first year.

As we became more knowledgeable about public relations strategies, our growing media exposure reached a diverse set of outlets. In the first couple of years, we had interviews with or articles in *The Toronto Globe and Mail*, *Redbook Magazine*, *The Washington Post*, *Bloomberg Business Radio*, *Montreal Gazette*, *American Legion Magazine*, *Dallas Morning News*, and *The Philadelphia Inquirer*. We also made numerous appearances on CSPAN and local radio stations in Columbus, Ohio; Washington, DC; Nashville; Boston; and New York City.

We quickly learned that, as Marshall McLuhan famously said, "The medium is the message," which meant we had to adapt our messages to fit the needs and practices of print and video journalists. They invariably listened for pithy statements that made for easy quotes, so we used words and phrases we believed would end up on the page or screen, such as "Where girls come first," "Girls schools are can-do environments," and "A counter-culture for girls." We found that simple statements like these resonated with the public we were trying to reach.

With an office in our home, I never knew when one of our children would pop into the room with a question or need. One time while being interviewed by *The New York Times*, I heard a heart-stopping scream. With the phone at my ear, I walked into the hallway to witness a fight over my daughter's favorite toy. Knowing that she, too, had heard that scream, I explained to the reporter that there was nothing to worry about—just a bit of sibling rivalry.

In time, I learned how to prepare effectively for live interviews on television or film. I made a point of wearing bright-colored jackets in red or teal. Not only were these colors more telegenic, but I felt more powerful in them than if I had worn a typical black business suit. I watched countless interviews to get examples of the most effective speaking techniques. They taught me not to insert audible pauses, like "uh," "ahh," or "er." If I was unsure of what to say next, I would hesitate silently until the right words came to me. I may not have been ready for prime time, but I did just fine.

As Meg and I developed our public relations materials, we sought to develop a vocabulary describing the girls' school experience and outcomes that could be used by others. The goal in all these efforts was to help member schools draw freely on what we had already researched and formulated rather than having to create their own versions.

In 1994, NCGS contracted with Anne Rosenfeld and her firm, Public Information Resources, Inc. (PIRI), to become our new public relations company. Anne and her team led us in new efforts that produced press releases, member surveys, tip sheets, media initiatives, and public relations strategies.

In the same period, we wrote, designed, and produced a variety of publications for use by our membership. In this work, we were blessed with the talents of graphic designer Sara Lennon, who collaborated with us on and off for 17 years. These items also served as informative marketing materials that we could use with a broader audience. We entitled our membership directory "Choosing A Girls' School." Along with a geographic index of member schools with their contact information, the 20-page edition contained photos, NCGS facts, and tips for how to pick a school. In addition to distributing the directory to member schools, we sent it out to more than 4,000 people in the NCGS database.

An early publication printed in 1993, entitled *What Every Girl in School Needs to Know* (affectionately called WAGS), became the Coalition's bestseller. Close to 50,000 copies were distributed in the first 18 months at a price of $1.50 per copy, creating a new revenue stream for us. Its success was best described by Arlene Gibson, head of Spence School in Manhattan at the time. She said during a winter board meeting, "The first time I opened the blue and black marbled notebook I felt tears in my eyes. The piece was a milestone for the NCGS membership. It was tangible evidence that we were accomplishing our major goal—telling the story of schools for girls."

Through our work with our member schools, we learned that parents of girls were thirsty for guidance. In response, we created and published *Raising Confident, Competent Daughters* and *Dads and Their Daughters* in the mid-1990s.

"The first time I opened the blue and black marbled notebook I felt tears in my eyes. The piece was a milestone for the NCGS membership. It was tangible evidence that we were accomplishing our major goal—telling the story of schools for girls."

ARLENE GIBSON
Former head of Spence School in Manhattan

A few of the NCGS publications used by member schools in recruitment efforts, developed and distributed as a service to members and available to them at cost.

These booklets were replete with tips for parents on how to encourage their daughters' interest in math and science, find ways to support their participation in team sports, and let them know they have the power to say what they think.

Another popular publication, *In the News*, rolled off the presses in 1995 and enjoyed a wide distribution. It contained reprinted news articles featuring Coalition stories, girls' issues, ongoing research, and profiles of girls' school alumnae. Many member schools put *In the News* in their Admissions waiting rooms to strengthen their competitive edge.

These publications provided additional sources of income for us as well as public exposure. To increase sales, we produced a two-color flyer listing the available materials. The initial run of 5,000 copies of this flyer ran out within the first six months. Requests poured in from across the country as well as from South Africa, Germany, Japan, Thailand, Saudi Arabia, and Korea. Before long, the three-piece series on *Girls, Math and Science* went into its second printing.

To complement these publications, PIRI created short public service advisory columns for parents on a selection of topics: *My Daughter, the Physicist* (math/science); the *Power of Peers* (relationships); *Your Daughter and Sports* (athletics); *Finding Her Voice* (self-esteem). Once again, these tip sheets appeared in multiple media markets, both in print and on television news shows.

In this pre–social media era, print publications and broadcast journalism were the mainstay of communication. In order to stay in the public eye, NCGS managed to find a way to join in whenever a girl-related topic or theme received local or national attention. We linked up with the International Day of the Girl, Girl Scouts of America events, Take Our Daughters to Work Day, other Ms. Foundation celebrations, Women's History Month, and Women in Sports Day. Our successful media campaigning, which took enormous energy and constant vigilance, ensured that all the hard work we were doing—and the vision, innovation, creativity, and commitment we were bringing to that work—would position NCGS in the forefront of the important advances being made in girls' education.

Why Girls' Schools Matter

Top (left to right): Whitty Ransome, Dr. Sally Ride, and Barbara Wagner, head of Marlborough School in Los Angeles. Dr. Ride, a girls' school graduate, spoke at the dedication of the new science facility at Marlborough School

Bottom: In 1999 Cokie Roberts was the NCGS Woman of Achievement. Left to right, Rebecca Fox, Meg Moulton, Diana Beebe, Cokie Roberts, Whitty Ransome

–XI–
Building an Entrepreneurial Enterprise

*Without boys, girls are empowered to speak up
and use their own voice. We are not only encouraged to
take on more responsibility but also to create
our own leadership positions.*

—ANNE, GRADE 11

From its inception, NCGS organized membership conferences and subject-specific programs. What became known as the NCGS Annual Conference, first held in June 1991, offered unique opportunities for girls' school leaders, because no other organization focused exclusively on girl-related issues. All our workshops, speakers, and materials were relevant to administrators, admissions directors, public relations specialists, and fundraising experts. The conference also offered job-specific professional development workshops for school teams. These cohorts were encouraged to return to their campuses with new knowledge and a commitment to working together to put the ideas into action.

At first, member schools hosted the conferences with participants sleeping in dorms. But these were rarely comfortable arrangements. June weather could be hot or cold, and student rooms were not known for their amenities. We earned the nickname "Cheap Chicks" for keeping costs down, but we didn't win any hospitality prizes.

Meg and I were strategic in our search for potential speakers at these conferences. We decided to create an award called Woman of Achievement to honor well-known women who were making a difference. With award winners as our keynote speakers, we attracted large, enthusiastic audiences eager to hear their words. Among our honorees were Judy Woodruff of the PBS Newshour; Dr. Helen Caldicott of Physicians for Social Responsibility; Cokie Roberts of ABC TV (who shared her recent book, *We Are Our Mothers' Daughters*); Dr. Rosabeth Moss Kanter from Harvard Business School; Dr. Sally Ride, one of the first women astronauts; Supreme Court Justice Ruth Bader Ginsburg; and Dr. Jane Goodall, the esteemed anthropologist. Other notable speakers at our conferences included Marty Evans, executive director of Girl Scouts of America; Marie Wilson, head of the Ms. for Women Foundation; Dr. Ruth Simmons, president of Brown University; Jackie Woods, executive director of the American Association of University Women; Dorothy Hamill, Olympic gold medalist in figure skating; and Isabel Stewart, head of Girls' Inc. You can imagine how these accomplished speakers, representing so many different walks of life, enlivened our annual gatherings and brought a wide breadth of knowledge and experience to the work we were doing together.

Recruiting these history-making women involved tapping the connections of member school leaders. Dr. Sally Ride graduated from Westlake School for Girls; Justice Ginsburg's daughter, Jane, went to Nightingale-Bamford in New York City; and Cokie Roberts' sister was cared for by a Sacred Heart School principal during her dying days. So, our speakers were familiar with all-girls educational models and brought their support with them.

I have especially vivid memories of three of our Women of Achievement. When Dr. Sally Ride was honored at our 2001 Annual Conference held in Washington, D.C., the room went silent as she rose to speak. Participants knew they had a treat in store and were in the presence of a history-maker. Dr. Ride began by showing a series of photos taken from inside her spaceship. Images of her floating around the cabin with other items flying through the air drew "ahs"

Building an Entrepreneurial Enterprise

"And may your schools thrive as you encourage the girls and young women in your charge to love learning and relish living, to aspire and to achieve, to make their communities, country and world a little better because they lived."

JUSTICE RUTH BADER GINSBURG

Above (left to right): Rachel Belash, Justice Ruth Bader Ginsburg, Mary Lou Leipheimer, and Arlene Gibson at the NCGS 10th Anniversary celebration in Washington, D.C. in 2001.

Right: Justice Ginsburg received the NCGS Woman of Achievement Award at the anniversary event.

and "oohs" from the audience. But when she shared pictures of Earth from outer space, her audience let out a collective gasp. If anyone still needed proof of the ways women can make a difference in the world of science and technology, this was it. Later that year, Dr. Ride, joined by three colleagues, would co-found Sally Ride Science, a program to promote equity and inclusion for all students, especially girls, in STEM (science, technology, engineering, and mathematics) studies and careers.

At the same Annual Conference, Justice Ruth Bader Ginsburg shared with us a paper she had written about the wives of Supreme Court justices. She noted that behind the scenes, these women would sometimes influence their husband's opinions and took particular note of Malvina Harlan, who urged her husband, John, to vote against the 1896 *Plessy v. Ferguson* decision, which upheld the "separate but equal" policy that perpetuated segregation laws. Though he was in the minority, Harlan's written dissent became a key element in the overturning of the decision in 1954. In her closing remarks, Justice Ginsburg left us with this charge: "May your schools thrive as you encourage girls and young women in your charge to love learning and love living, to aspire and to achieve, to make their communities, country, and world a little better because they lived."

Several years later, we had a much different presentation from our awardee, Dr. Jane Goodall. Unable to attend in person, she accepted her Woman of Achievement Award via video. She made a few comments but then let out an ear-shattering simulated call of a wild gorilla. The audience—stunned to silence—slowly rose and applauded Dr. Goodall's unusual acceptance gesture. What a rallying call that was!

The Annual Conference fees generated close to $20,000 in net revenue each year. Yet as a young and growing nonprofit, we were always on the hunt for much-needed revenue to support our programmatic goals. We soon learned that subject-specific conferences, such as Girls and the Physical Sciences and Girls and Technology, had wide appeal. Part of the attraction had to do with the hands-on activities that made up many of these conference sessions. A number of the tips for teachers evolved from conference participants' tinkering with materials to build items such as go-carts, bridges, and merry-go-rounds. The lessons learned from these projects became the source for publications that we sold to member schools and the general public as a way to get girls engaged in creative engineering.

To fully fund the Girls and Technology conference, NCGS applied for a National Science Foundation grant of $75,000 to underwrite the production and distribution of the booklets for teachers and parents along with a video that included a resource guide. We were thrilled when we received that grant, which validated our work and our vision.

NCGS also partnered with Google in 2006 for an "Introduce a Girl to Engineering Day" in New York City. Later that year, we connected with Dr. Maria Klawe, dean of the School of Engineering and Applied Science at Princeton University, who organized another session on girls and engineering on her campus. Our work was fueled by a strong belief that getting girls interested in fields such as engineering, architecture, and construction could expand their career horizons.

Role models were hard to find, though, and I knew I wasn't in a position to serve in that capacity. But I needed to be knowledgeable enough to serve as a spokesperson on these subjects. Perhaps it was only a symbolic gesture, but I made what I considered a bold move and rented the Boston Computer Museum for my 50th birthday party. Friends displayed an array of photos from my life, and these hung alongside pictures of computer pioneers, including a few women. I definitely did not have a place among them! When I made my "thank you for coming" speech, I explained why the locale had significance for me. I told the guests that when something went wrong with technology, I would blame the poor instructions or a faulty piece of equipment. I never said to myself that it could have been my lack of knowledge that was at fault. Choosing the Computer Museum to mark this birthday was an acknowledgment that I had to move out of my comfort zone when it came to technology. This seemed like a good place to start—and to state my resolve in public.

Some of this new resolve was a legacy from my upbringing. I came from a business-based family. My grandfather, Percy Allen Ransome, started a Caterpillar Tractor dealership back in the early 1900s. For 25 years my father, Percy Allen Ransome Jr., served as president of the construction equipment company that became known as Giles and Ransome. Although I received no encouragement to pursue a corporate career, I learned a lot around the dinner table. I began reading the business section of our local paper, *The Boston Globe*. At first, I understood perhaps 10 percent of what I read, but that ratio gradually improved, especially when I focused on companies I knew by name, like Coca-Cola, CVS, IBM, and Marshalls. Over time, I became fairly well versed in business language and practices.

As a result, even though my technology skills needed honing, my early lessons in what made businesses run and thrive served as a good basis for approaching corporate entities to ask for their support, which we needed to supplement our income from dues, publication sales, and conference fees. With a budget based on dues of $8.50 per student, with a $1,500 minimum and $5,200 maximum membership fee, we needed a broader base of revenue to finance some of our more ambitious goals. I thought we stood a good chance of securing sponsorships if we approached the businesses that had service contracts with our member schools. We designed a survey for member schools that included questions about the vendors they used for food services, retirement accounts, computer programs, consultants, uniforms, sports equipment, textbooks, banking, etc. With specific data in hand about relationships between member schools and their suppliers, I approached business representatives seeking sponsorship support for a project or a conference. As a result, Google gave us funds to redesign our website; TIAA-CREF underwrote an annual conference reception; and First Republic Bank helped launch our financial literacy for girls programming.

I loved making these solicitations because I thought of them less as fundraising ventures and more as advocacy for the important work we were doing for girls around the country. I believed we were good partners for these corporate sponsors. Our schools gave them a lot of business each year, and sponsoring our programs would ensure sustained relationships moving forward.

When NCGS reached our 10-year anniversary early in the new millennium, conference fees, foundation grants, publication sales, and corporate sponsorships constituted a solid financial base for our work. It was time to look ahead at growing our programming and, perhaps, trading our home offices for more professional digs.

–XII–
Transitions and Celebrations: 2000–01

*The confidence your school gives you and
the atmosphere of being with all girls is amazing because
they support you and challenge you.*

—ALANNA, GRADE 10

After 19 years as Concord Academy's head of school, my husband, Tom Wilcox, left in June 2000 to accept the presidency of the Baltimore Community Foundation. When Tom was first offered the position, I was dead set against leaving the Boston area and was busy exploring possible rentals in Concord. But Wally Pinkard, board president of the foundation, put on a full-court press to show me why coming to Baltimore would be a good move for me, too. Tom and I went on a two-day trip to explore the possibilities of moving south that included private tours of the two sports stadiums: Camden Yards, home of the Orioles major-league baseball team, and what is now M and T stadium, home of the National Football League's Ravens. I enjoyed a luncheon with local women leaders, met with a realtor who showed us houses that cost a fraction of what we could get in the Boston area. I also visited Bryn Mawr School, whose head, Rebecca Fox, showed me a space she said I could use as a possible office. This would be in addition to what I might organize at our home. I also received a call from Peter O'Neill, head of Garrison Forest School, who extolled the benefits of moving to Baltimore. Peter and I had been friends for years, going back to our days as admissions directors. He told me there were more than eight girls' schools in the Baltimore area, so I would have plenty of colleagues. By the time Tom and I returned to Concord, I was sold on the move.

Our final year at Concord Academy was filled with emotional endings and plans for new beginnings. We enjoyed a host of farewell celebrations in major cities, including New York, Washington, D.C., Philadelphia, San Francisco, Los Angeles, and Chicago. Revisiting highlights of our time at the school made for a busy and exciting series of events.

At the same time, I remained committed to my work as co-executive director of NCGS, so a major question for me involved how to transition away from the second-floor bedroom in the head's house. which had served as the official NCGS headquarters since 1991. We used my home office as the Coalition's mailing address as well, even though Meg kept a home office, too. Once I moved to Baltimore, I wondered, where would we locate our central office, and how could Meg and I make our partnership work from two different locations?

For several years, we had managed to run the organization on our own. But it became clear, as NCGS grew and activities increased, that we needed help. So in 1995, we had hired Concord Academy staff member Sue Sauer as a part-time administrative assistant who came to my house each day. When she left in 1998, we were fortunate to bring Ann Parke on board to serve as a full-time director of administrative services. As I prepared to move, we began our search for a new home for NCGS, and Meg, Ann, and I turned our attention to how we planned to reorganize our work. Board members had often praised our ability to stay nimble and adaptable, and those habits helped us work together smoothly while considering new administrative models. Advances in technology made a big difference, of course. The growth of the internet, email, websites, and telecommunication offered us new ways of staying connected. Though remote working arrangements are common practice today, they were still relatively rare at the time, especially in tiny nonprofits. As it turned out, we didn't find professional office space until January 2001, six months after I had left for Baltimore. So for those six months—before Ann moved into our new administrative office at 57

Main Street in Concord—we made good use of technology and travel to keep things moving without interruption. Although I now worked remotely, I made frequent trips to Concord, where we would gather for meetings. Conference calls kept us in touch as well.

This transition period actually became the busiest and most fruitful year NCGS had experienced to that point. Meg and I connected almost every week. Our to-do lists were colorful and decorated with graphic images of topics we needed to discuss. I traveled often with Meg to member gatherings in cities around the country, including San Francisco, Los Angeles, Cleveland, Baltimore, Providence, Philadelphia, Boston, and D.C. These sessions focused on sharing information about the latest research, publications, enrollment challenges, and media opportunities. In 2001 we switched to an independent contractor for our public relations and publications work. Carolyn Colletti brought with her a broad understanding of how to work with the media and considerable talent with graphic design, which enhanced our outreach efforts in creative and significant ways.

Meanwhile, the 10th anniversary of NCGS's founding was coming up in June 2001, and we were planning to hold the event in Washington, D.C. We were all pointing to that moment, which would celebrate a successful first decade of membership growth and expanding awareness of the value of our mission. Since 1991, member schools had grown from 56 to 97. More important, overall enrollments at girls' schools had increased by 37% with 68% of schools at capacity, almost triple the levels of our founding year.

A serendipitous encounter brought us a splendid opportunity for our 10th anniversary. We hosted an opening event at the Smithsonian Museum with sports journalist Jane Gottesman and photographer Geoffrey Biddle. For years, the team of Gottesman and Biddle had collected photos of girls and women participating in athletic endeavors through organized sports and simpler forms of exercise, such as jumping rope, hopscotch, and roller-skating. Gottesman recognized the dearth of media coverage for girls and women in sports and saw the need for a book that honored both top female athletes and everyday girls and women whose self-image was strengthened through athletic participation. The pair titled their proposed book and activities packet *Game Face: What Does*

On the inside title page of *Game Face: What Does a Female Athlete Look Like*, a red seal celebrates NCGS's 10th anniversary along with a reference to the Foreword by actor/director Penny Marshall.

a Female Athlete Look Like? The collection of images illustrated the diversity of body types and pursuits that offered freedom from traditional feminine constraints and explored the emotional pleasures of competition and play.

I suggested that Penny Marshall, director of the film *A League of Their Own*, be approached to write a foreword for the book, and we were all delighted when she agreed. When the book was published, we were also thrilled at the glowing endorsements, including these three:

> Whether you're from the generation of drum majorettes or Title IX, the athletes of *Game Face* will inspire you. For women to become strong is a deep part of the revolution.
> —*Gloria Steinem*

> *Game Face* is a first. Together these photographs give a face to the critical mass of people who made women's sports part of the popular culture.
> —*Billie Jean King*

> These images are striking, distinctive, and evocative. Over the past generation, many of us arrived at a better understanding of what athletic participation can mean to girls and women. *Game Face* heightens that understanding.
> —*Bob Costas, NBC Sports*

Transitions and Celebrations: 2000–2001

A collage of historic and contemporary images from *Game Face: What Does a Female Athlete Look Like*.

Group of current and former NCGS board members in 2001.
Back Row, left to right: Burch Ford, Rachel Belash, Mary Lou Leipheimer, Meg Moulton; front row, left to right: Diana Beebe, Aggie Underwood, Olive Long, Whitty Ransome, and Arlene Gibson.

Leading up to the Smithsonian photography exhibit and book launch, NCGS served as an appropriate partner in the *Game Face* effort, and we worked side by side with the authors in the pursuit of corporate sponsors. Mass Mutual Financial Group and its subsidiary, Oppenheimer Funds, Inc., became the primary underwriters of the project. The most exciting aspect of this collaboration for us was the inclusion of NCGS on the inside title page with the statement "Celebrating the Tenth Anniversary of the National Coalition of Girls' Schools," along with a prominent sticker with the same message. As an act of appreciation and support, member schools purchased a total of 250 copies of the book to give to families, speakers, alumnae, and donors. NCGS also promoted a traveling show of *Game Face* with teaching materials and an array of photos from the book to use as illustrations.

As a lifetime athlete, I took special pleasure in the *Game Face* project. In high school, I played varsity field hockey, basketball, and lacrosse, my favorite team sport. I was captain of the lacrosse team my senior year and high scorer during my four-year career on our undefeated team. I came from a family of athletes, with a father and an uncle who became star college lacrosse players

Transitions and Celebrations: 2000–2001

Top to bottom: Moorestown Friends School graduation awards; the 1963 undefeated varsity lacrosse team with Whitty to the left of Coach Floss Brudon; Whitty in full swing on the way to winning the 1962 Philadelphia Junior Golf tournament.

at Princeton. I actually learned a few scoring tricks from my uncle, Ernie Ransome, who made the U.S. All-American Team. My favorite individual sport, though, was golf, and it still is. I came from a long line of golfers that included my grandmother, father, mother, aunt, and uncle. I played competitively in junior tournaments in my area and won the South Jersey tournament at 15 and the Philadelphia Junior Championship at 17. My uncle and I also won the Philadelphia Griscom Cup two years in a row. I still play as often as I can, but I'm not as good as I once was. My memories of that momentous 10th Anniversary show are happy reminders that I was fortunate to have had the experience of being a young female athlete and then be able to support future generations of female athletes everywhere. I still cherish a letter I received from Jane Gottesman several years after the event in which she wrote, "I will never think of *Game Face* without thinking of you in the next breath. You were involved and supportive of *Game Face* well before we were—what good instincts!"

When I look back at that action-packed year, I'm amazed at all we were able to accomplish in the midst of so much change. From an organizational perspective, it felt as though NCGS had come of age and was here to stay. For me personally, the need to keep focusing on the organization helped ease my transition to a new home. It wasn't easy for Tom and me to leave a place we loved, a place where we had welcomed and raised two children. But my work at NCGS remained a centering place for me, demanding my attention and creativity and allowing me to stay connected to Concord in a way that didn't dwell in the past but kept pointing me toward the future.

–XIII–
Let's Talk About Money

Teachers are very conscious that they are teaching at an all-girls' school. They not only want to teach us academic subjects, they are also invested in helping us grow as young women.

—CARMEN, GRADE 12

I first learned about an exciting program called Camp $tart-Up when its associate director, Melinda Little, asked for a meeting in 1996. I was intrigued from the start and sensed there could be a valuable partnership between its parent organization, Independent Means, Inc., and NCGS. The camp taught girls about personal finance and the importance that financial literacy would have in their lives. They learned how to build a business, design a product or service, create a marketing and sales plan, and estimate profit and loss. I had not yet thought about financial literacy as another component of a girl's education, but this program made me see how relevant it was.

    I remember my first introduction to the topic of money, in particular the stock market. My fifth-grade teacher, Mr. Blyer, had us read the business section of the daily newspaper looking for possible investment opportunities. I'm not sure why I picked Standard Oil of New Jersey, but I asked my dad to buy me a share, and he readily agreed. I loved looking at the rise and fall in the price of my share. Over the years, it became Esso and then Exxon. Though I didn't hold on to that share, I have continued to invest and watch with interest the ups and downs of the market.

There is no question that learning one's ABCs is essential. But what an oversight not to include a D for dollars! We all remember the fairy tales. The damsels in distress always managed to find a Prince Charming to come to their rescue. Yet happy-ever-after endings aren't so easy to come by in real life. Women will spend at least one-third of their lives on their own, and eight out of ten will manage their own money at some point. I was learning that financial understanding was the next step in the evolution toward true gender equity. When girls and women learn about money—earn it, manage it, invest it, and give it competently and confidently— the economic playing field becomes a level one. That had not yet happened at the time, and though we are getting closer today, we are not all the way there yet.

My mentor and guru for this new way of thinking was Joline Godfrey, president of Independent Means, Inc., and author of *No More Frogs To Kiss: 99 Ways to Give Economic Power to Girls*; *Raising Financially Fit Kids*; and *20 $ecrets to Money and Independence*. Godfrey talked about financial literacy as being similar to learning a new language. She wanted girls to develop a "Dollar Diva"

Joline Godfrey, president of Independent Means, Inc., is honored as a NCGS Woman of Achievement in 2005. Her book, *No More Frogs to Kiss*, with a foreword by Gloria Steinem, helped those wanting to encourage financial literacy among girls.

checklist, which included setting goals on growing a savings account, balancing a checkbook, negotiating payment for a job, budgeting wisely, investing in stocks, bonds, and money market funds, and getting comfortable talking about money. She spoke at several of NCGS's annual conferences and helped us design workshops for students, parents, and teachers that we organized throughout the country for member schools. First Republic Bank served as our major underwriter for regional workshops in Baltimore, Boston, Honolulu, New York City, San Francisco, and Washington, D.C.

In 2000, our work on financial literacy culminated in a national conference titled Girls, Women, and Money. On the last page of the conference booklet was a letter on White House stationery from President Bill Clinton, with this message:

> I commend the organizers and participants of this event for promoting financial empowerment and economic literacy for women and girls. By contributing to their professional, educational, and economic advancement, you are helping a new generation of leaders to make their own important contributions to the life of our nation and the strength of our economy. Hillary joins me in extending best wishes for a productive conference and every success in your efforts. (See page 101.)

The titles of conference sessions offer a broad view of the topics addressed during this three-day event. They included The Psychology of Money; The Entrepreneurial Instinct; E-Business Is She Business; What Are You Worth?: The Dynamics of Negotiating; Avenues of Economic Justice; and Why Women Give Differently Than Men, among others. There were 500 attendees, and exchanges during breaks and meals offered them a chance to share ideas and strategies.

As with NCGS's other major conferences, a series of publications followed. They included *Money $ense for Girls: A Resource Guide for Parents and Educators*; and *Money $ense: A Guide for Girls*, a booklet featuring media articles on the conference along with lists of tips on how to take charge of money matters. We also produced a wallet-size *Spending Diary* to track daily expenditures. That conference enjoyed broad media coverage, including a front-page article in *The New York Times* and pieces in *The Boston Globe*, *The Christian Science Monitor*, and *San Francisco Chronicle*.

My favorite article on the topic appeared in *The Baltimore Sun*. The headline asked, "Have You Had the Talk? The One About Money?" Rather than referring to *that* talk—the one about menstruation, female bodies, and sex—the piece offered helpful tips for parents as they talked with their daughters about money matters.

The best sign that we were making a difference in this important area was the commitment by individual member schools to teach girls financial literacy within their existing curriculums. They began to ask where money lessons could be taught within history, literature, art, math, science, music, and other departments. Numerous schools brought Joline Godfrey to campus to talk with faculty, parents, and trustees about the critical nature of financial education, urging all in attendance to find ways to help the young women they parented and taught to advance their financial literacy skills.

I may have been a bit slow to catch on to the importance of money in the lives of girls and women, despite my own interest as a young girl, but I was happy to learn from Joline Godfrey's inspiring work and delighted that others were learning along with me.

–XIV–
The Global Road

My girls' school experience prepared me to put my best self forward and dive into new experiences at university.

— JESSLEY, GRADUATE

Three weeks after my marriage to Tom Wilcox in 1979, I boarded a plane for Saudi Arabia. Unlike many of my high school and college friends, I had never traveled across the Atlantic, and I never would have guessed I'd be going to such exotic lands.

In my role as director of admissions at Dana Hall School, I had been invited by the Arab American Oil Company (ARAMCO) on an all-expense-paid trip to Saudi Arabia, the United Arab Emirates, and Kuwait. At the time of my adventure, American children of ARAMCO employees had to leave the country after eighth grade to attend a boarding school back in the United States. Aware of the stereotypical behavior of American teenagers, the ARAMCO leadership seemed to believe that these adolescents were best sent off to school elsewhere, which would perhaps alleviate the possibility that they would engage in mischief or misconduct in a strict Muslim country. So my role was to present the benefits of attending Dana Hall to prospective parents and female students.

On the flight to Dhahran, I was the only Westerner and the only woman. Since I didn't speak any language other than English, I was worried that I wouldn't find the help I needed if anything should happen during the trip. Fortunately, the flight went as planned with no unusual incidents.

I still have the detailed notebook that my assistant at Dana Hall had prepared for me. While many of the pages have yellowed with age, the contents make for an interesting read. I spent my first three days in Dhahran, where I made four presentations to prospective applicant families, and four girls enrolled at Dana as a result. Wherever I traveled in the country, I had to be accompanied by a man and dress conservatively.

My travels took me next to Riyadh and Jeddah in Saudi Arabia, then to Dubai and Abu Dhabi. I stayed with American parents whose children still attended ARAMCO schools. Today, Dubai and Abu Dhabi are considered Westernized in their architecture, economies, and commercial establishments, and have become popular tourist meccas. But in 1979, these countries had yet to put their oil riches to work on modernization, so I was amazed by some of the sights: vast desert roads, abandoned tractors and trucks along the way, and camels wandering by.

My final destination on the recruiting trip was meant to be Kuwait, but that leg was canceled due to disruptions in that country. Instead, I flew to Rome, where I met Tom for a delayed honeymoon. We continued through Europe with stops in Florence, Lugano, Paris, and London. At last, I had had an international experience, and what a varied one it was!

This first experience in international travel was followed by other personal trips, and these served as a great prelude to the travel I would do for my work with NCGS. My first official trip abroad on behalf of the Coalition came in response to an invitation Meg and I received in 1996 from the Girls School Association of Great Britain. They asked us to come to London and speak about how we had organized a coalition of girls' schools with a mission of increasing visibility and enrollments. This trip not only allowed us to share our expertise with our British counterparts but also to invite their association to become an affiliate member of NCGS, which they eventually did.

Meg and I had earlier traveled to Canada on an informal mission to learn about common causes, and we established meaningful collaborations with girls' schools there through our relationship with the Canadian Accredited Independent Schools (CAIS), so our trip to London was another extension of our growing outreach efforts.

The Global Road

In 1998, Meg heard from a group of girls' schools in Australia hoping she would attend an informal gathering of their national alliance. The relations with our Down Under sister schools became a prime focus for Meg. She returned to the country often and encouraged their attendance at our different conferences. The Aussie leaders traveled around the world on a regular basis, and when they were in the U.S., Meg enjoyed helping with their itineraries and offering introductions to key leaders in the girls' school world that we knew so well. She also loved giving visitors tours of Concord. On her drives through town, she would point to 228 Main Street, the imposing Victorian-style house where

Right: Meg Moulton, Gillian DuCharme, head of the Girls School Association of England, and Whitty Ransome, during Meg and Whitty's visit to London to speak about successful NCGS strategies that could benefit schools everywhere.

Below: The International Girls' Forum panel with various NCGS leaders in the back row.

our Concord Academy office resided, exclaiming that it was the international headquarters of NCGS! Over time, Meg brought Australia, New Zealand, Canada, England, and South Africa into the NCGS fold as affiliate members.

A few of our annual conferences developed international themes as well, and in 2002 we honored Tajwar Kakar, founder of the Primary School of Hope in Afghanistan, as our Woman of Achievement. A major speaker at that gathering was Louise Richardson, a world expert on terrorism. We also heard from Ann Cotton, founder of CAMFED, a pan-African association promoting education for girls and women. Cotton spoke of her work in Ghana helping marginalized girls finish secondary school and supporting transition programs that helped young women move into further education and training.

At that 2002 Annual Conference, NCGS brought together girls from the United States, Canada, Australia, South Africa, and New Zealand to serve on our inaugural International Girls' Forum. Two girls from each country tackled issues of international significance and discussed their suggestions for improving the lives of women within their own countries. Following the conference, the participating girls kept in touch and vowed to continue doing good things in their countries and around the world. A year later, the Australian Alliance invited girls from these same countries to a student conference in Sydney. Ten girls from the U.S. attended and presented their thoughts on "Building the Next Generation of Leaders." In 2004 and 2005, other students from U.S. girls' schools joined their international counterparts on panels here in the U.S. and in Canada.

As a result of these decades-long efforts, in June 2022 NCGS expanded its scope and became the International Coalition of Girls' Schools (ICGS). Less than two years later, ICGS included 550 member schools in 23 countries. Enrollments at these schools totaled more than 350,000 students. From a fledging cohort in 1991, our coalition of schools had grown into a powerful network that reached around the world.

–XV–
A New Decade: The 2000s

*One of the most important things about
the environment of a girls' school is you are encouraged
to take risks and try new things*

—RONNIE, GRADE 11

The 10th anniversary of NCGS in 2001 enjoyed the highest overall ratings of any annual conference up to that year. How could it not with luminaries like Supreme Court Justice Ruth Bader Ginsburg and Astronaut Dr. Sally Ride as featured speakers?

Once the conference wrapped up, Meg and I moved on with our work. As legendary publisher Katharine Graham once said, "To love what you do and feel that it matters—how could anything be more fun?" We certainly loved what we did. We were being shown that it mattered. And we were having fun doing it.

At this stage, the work involved an expanding focus on girls and financial literacy, harnessing the internet to facilitate and broaden communication, and serving as resources for members, parents, students, and educators. In September 2002, NCGS launched a redesigned website with greatly expanded electronic communication potential.

One of the most exciting developments during this time came from the founding of new girls' public schools that joined the two existing ones. In 2002, five of our member schools came from the public sector: Chicago Young Women's Leadership Charter School, Jefferson Leadership Academy (CA), Philadelphia

High School for Girls, Western High School (Baltimore), and the Young Women's Leadership School (N.Y.C.).

Our annual conferences continued to draw participants from all over the U.S. and abroad. Offering job-specific breakout groups held particular appeal, as issues around the use of technology, the need for fundraising, and ongoing enrollment challenges called for an array of new approaches.

Unlike during the earliest years of NCGS, a plethora of books about girls and their development emerged in the 2000s, including research on the female brain. Two books published in 2002, Dr. JoAnn Deak's *Girls Will Be Girls; Raising Confident and Courageous Daughters* and Karen Stabiner's *All Girls: Single-Sex Education and Why It Matters* merited special attention. In response, NCGS organized more than 20 educational forums around the country during 2002–03 to spread their important messages. At public discussions moderated by Meg or me, Deak and Stabiner presented their research on what makes single-sex schooling an important option, especially for girls. With the participation of 55 member schools, close to 3,500 families gathered in Atlanta, Baltimore, Boston, Cleveland, Dallas, Honolulu, Los Angeles, New York City., Philadelphia, Richmond, San Francisco, Seattle, and Washington, D.C. to hear what they had to say.

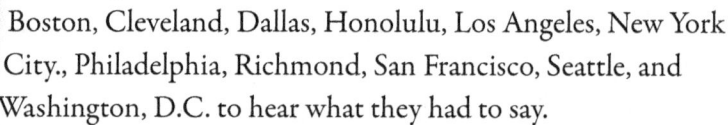

As I look back on these widespread gatherings, I recall that "on the road" served as our mantra during these early years of NCGS's second decade. Not only did we help organize the Deak-Stabiner authors' tour, we also expanded our financial literacy initiatives to cities around the country in areas with a cluster of member schools. Our lead sponsor for these seminars was First Republic Bank.

As our programming expanded, we needed to increase the support we received from corporations and foundations with like-minded missions. I loved pursuing such support, and I often compared the wooing of outside dollars to a courtship that led to a mutually satisfying merger of interests and benefits. Over time we received backing from the Klingenstein Foundation; Sodexho; Carney,

Sandoe, and Associates; Educational Outfitters; Marts & Lundy; Educational Directions; TIAA-CREF; SAGE Dining; Blackbaud; and Whipple Hill, among others. In one year alone, we amassed $60,000 in external financial backing. For our small nonprofit, that amount made a significant difference in our ability to thrive.

Additional energies went to ongoing STEM activities. including a partnership with the National Engineers Week Foundation, which was tied to the PBS series "Design Squad." Meg kept the global work going by leading sessions in England, Australia, Canada, and South Africa. And NCGS continued to make regular appearances in media outlets, including *Newsweek*, *The Wall Street Journal*, *Forbes.com*, *Teen Vogue*, *USA Today*, *The Seattle Times*, and *The Baltimore Sun*. A front-page article about girls and financial literacy that appeared in *The New York Times* became the centerpiece of our annual tabloid publication, *In the News*.

In June 2004, the annual conference went to San Francisco. My excitement for our first western gathering was mainly fueled by one of our major speakers, Anne Lamott, author of *Bird by Bird: Some Instructions on Writing and Life* and *Traveling Mercies: Some Thoughts on Faith*. Lamott's writing inspired me, and her reflections on writing were generously sprinkled with humor and wisdom. She told us that the title *Bird by Bird* grew from a conversation her father had had with her younger brother. He had been given a school assignment about birds and felt overwhelmed by the task. "Where do I start?" he cried to their father. His response said it all: "The only way to do this is bird by bird." South African theologian Desmond Tutu had given a similar response in favor of patience and perseverance when asked how one might eat an elephant: "[A] bite at a time," he wisely replied. Lamott's comments at the conference didn't disappoint, and I have a favorite picture of the two of us that I still cherish.

During this first decade of the new millennium, the issue of girls and technology was becoming a vital topic throughout the country. In 2006, NCGS developed a good relationship with Google as a result of their support for the Introduce a Girl to Engineering workshop we held that year in one of their New

Anne Lamott (left), acclaimed writer of *Bird by Bird*, *Traveling Mercies*, and many other bestsellers, with one of her biggest fans at the NCGS Annual Conference in San Francisco in 2004.

York City offices. The 60 girls who attended were wowed not only by the busy office culture and all the technology it was wielding, but also by the M&M candy dispenser, the fitness room loaded with the latest equipment, and the climbing wall where employees could test their skills during off moments. We were all thrilled when Google provided NCGS with $15,000 to upgrade the Girls and Technology section of our website.

Another important issue for us was leadership. Since the founding of NCGS, cultivating good leadership in member schools was an important part of our work. We knew that positive female role models, visionary thinkers, and creative innovators would lead girls' schools in ways that would ensure the best possible outcomes for their students. We were committed to helping schools find and nurture great leaders. In fact, one of our former board members, Joan Countryman, who headed the all-girls' K–12 Lincoln School in Rhode Island for 12 years until her retirement in 2005, was called upon in 2006 to become a consultant and interim head of the newly established Oprah Winfrey Leadership Academy for Girls in South Africa. The boarding school, founded with the support of former South African President Nelson Mandela, serves disadvantaged girls who would not otherwise have the chance to grow up into leaders. At the time of the school's founding, Oprah was quoted in a Reuters article as saying, "When you educate a girl, you begin to change the face of a nation."

To enhance our own efforts at leadership training among NCGS member schools, we partnered with Simmons School of Management in Boston on three occasions to organize Strategic Leadership Institutes for Experienced Women Educators. These seminars offered professional development opportunities for the women running our member schools, and they were met with great enthusiasm.

In all of these initiatives Carolyn Colletti, our public relations director, kept finding ways to attract media coverage. When we dedicated a month to the topic of financial literacy, offering templates for press releases that could be sent to local media outlets, she facilitated an appearance for me on "ABC News Now." The 15-minute interview aired during the show "Top Priority," hosted that day by "20/20" anchor Deborah Roberts. Such prominent media attention highlighted how important our work was in a world that was opening up to girls and women in unprecedented ways. The fact that we—and our member schools and their students—were getting noticed and celebrated not only helped raise awareness of our mission but also buoyed us as we charted our way forward.

Someone once said that NCGS "outperformed capacity." In other words, we were over-achievers. They suggested that four full-time staff members and one part-time employee managed to produce more programs, publications, activities, and visibility than many groups with double the staff. For me, though, the work continued to be driven by passion, and I rarely felt overextended. "To love what you do and feel that it matters—how could anything be more fun?"

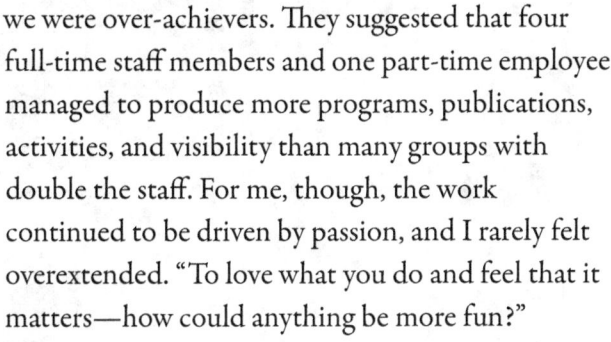

Far right: Joan Countryman (left) with Oprah Winfrey in August 2006, preparing for the opening of Oprah's Leadership Academy for Girls in South Africa;

Right: Nelson Mandela, former president of South Africa, speaking at the school's opening in 2007.

Why Girls' Schools Matter

Scenes from the 2008 Annual Conference and Whitty's farewell party.
Clockwise from top left: Jim Steyer, author of *The Other Parent: The Inside Story of the Media's Effect on Our Children*; Diana Beebe, head of Holton Arms School; two conference participants; Meg Moulton; Thomas E. Wilcox, Whitty's husband and former head of Concord Academy; and Bill Christ, head of Hathaway Brown School, with Whitty Ransome.

–XVI–
Leave Taking

I've learned to be both passionate and compassionate with everything I do.

—RONNIE, GRADE 11

In 2005, I began my own new decade. As I moved into my 60s, I wondered what I wanted to do with my life and career going forward. I had been working for different configurations of girls' school coalitions for nearly 20 years. I still enjoyed my work with NCGS, my outstanding colleagues, and the flexibility of my job. Yet I was beginning to feel that I had one more new venture in my bones. I didn't know what it might be or where it might take me, but as I thought about the years ahead, I felt it would be good to travel less, be closer to home, and connect with girls more directly.

It took a couple of years for me to decide how to act on these feelings, and I ended up announcing my desire to retire from NCGS in the fall of 2007, effective July 1, 2008. It came as a bit of a surprise since I had not hinted of the possibility while I was making up my mind. At one point, Meg and I had thought we'd leave at the same time, having shepherded NCGS through its early years and into a strong position to thrive without us. But I became ready sooner than Meg, who would leave in 2009, and the dovetailing of our departures allowed a more gradual transition into new leadership.

My final year was a very busy one for both of us, as we kept striving to enhance our programming and bring our message to more schools and families.

Here is a sampling of what kept that year so rich and fulfilling:

- Meg continued to travel abroad strengthening our contacts in England, Australia, New Zealand, and South Africa.
- We both made presentations at national gatherings of independent schools.
- The International Girls Forum convened for the fifth time at the June 2008 Annual Conference.
- A member services survey garnered strong support for NCGS's ability to deliver value through professional development workshops that highlighted best practices.
- $34,000 in non-dues revenue was added to the NCGS bottom line.
- A STEM Site-Within-A-Site on the Coalitions' website received major funding from Google.
- NCGS continued to appear in national and regional media outlets.
- Our expanded website became the online publishing arm of the girls' school community. Member schools were encouraged to share stories and accomplishments using the concept "Be the Media."

A particular highlight of my final year was a significant research project we embarked on with the help of Dr. Linda Sax from the UCLA Graduate School of Education and Information Studies. This project focused on female students from single-sex and coeducational independent high schools. Drawing from data collected in the well-respected Freshman Survey, an annual nationwide study of students entering their first year of college published by the Higher Education Research Institute (HERI), our study compared backgrounds, behaviors, attitudes, and aspirations of women who graduated from independent all girls' schools with women who had attended independent coed schools.

The key findings revealed good news for NCGS. Girls' school graduates rated their confidence in their abilities higher than their coed counterparts had done in the areas of math, computer skills, academic performance, self-confidence, public speaking, and writing. Additionally, girls' school graduates were more likely to pursue careers in engineering, consider graduate school, and be politically engaged. The final results of the UCLA study became available in the fall of 2008, after my July departure, but I read the outcome of the research with great pleasure. The analysis of the results gave additional weight to the NCGS mantra that girls' schools make a difference.

During all of this work, the Board was sorting out how to structure the management team following my departure. It was decided that Meg would assume the role of sole executive director for 2008–09. Kitty Burns, who had worked part time on special projects for five years, became director of member programs and corporate sponsorships, and Ann Parke, an NCGS staff member for 10 years, became director of member and administrative services. This superb group of women offered strong leadership and deep experience with our organization and its mission. In addition, the Board created a transition team to oversee ongoing strategic planning and generative thinking and planning, which was chaired by Ann Pollina of Westover School in Connecticut.

The 2008 Annual Conference at Hathaway Brown School in Cleveland served as the locale for my farewell to my NCGS colleagues and friends. Kitty Burns and Ann Parke were instrumental in organizing an unexpected series of gestures and celebratory events during our three days together. These included a series of remarks from Burch Ford, head of Miss Porter's School in Connecticut; Dorothy Hutchinson, head of Nightingale Bamford School in New York; and Meg Moulton, my partner in crime. Their words brought me to tears and taught me again that all our work together was changing lives for the better. When you are working hard and always pointing to the next strategy, the next project, the next goal, you can lose sight of the humanity involved in such work, and these women had the grace and wisdom to point it out.

I was also surprised and happy to receive a scrapbook with letters from former colleagues and friends. But the biggest surprise of all happened when my husband, Tom Wilcox, got up to speak. He shared with my colleagues that I had been considered as a candidate to head Concord Academy, explained the partnership role I took on when he accepted the job, described how we always made it a priority to spend time with our two children, Kate and Chris, and acknowledged the balancing act I had had to play. He mentioned, too, that I had always voiced my appreciation for the board leadership of NCGS and spoke about how blessed I had been to follow my passion as a girls' school revolutionary, never feeling it was work. Finally, Tom announced that he had created an endowed award called "The Ransome Prize" to honor my commitment to NCGS. The annual recipient would be chosen by the NCGS board and given to a girl or woman who had uniquely committed herself to the lives of other girls and women. (See page 100 for prize winners to date.) He asked that the nominees reflect pure devotion to a higher cause, the willingness to serve others, and the grace and readiness to credit the accomplishments of others, qualities he said he had always seen in me. As one friend said, it felt like a public love letter. What a beautiful note on which to end my tenure at NCGS.

It was, of course, a bittersweet departure, but I knew I had to let go in order to move on. And that feeling in my bones was assuring me that other exciting ventures lay ahead.

Tom and Whitty after the farewell party in 2008.

–XVII–
Continuing the Work

The all-girls experience has taught me a lot about self-advocacy. It's up to me to initiate change and to realize my goals and dreams.

—SKYE GRADE 11

I left for vacation right after my final days at NCGS. My family traveled to our cottage in Canada, where I could unwind after a hectic last year. I was pleased with our many accomplishments during my 20 years of service, and I was confident that Meg and her team would do a great job taking the organization forward. At this point, though, I was already absorbed in planning for my next steps. Several months before my departure, I had had an unexpected conversation about a new opportunity. When I first entertained thought of leaving NCGS, I never would have guessed that I'd soon be involved in three start-up projects close to home that would occupy me over the next 10 years. It didn't seem that long ago that NCGS was a start-up project, and I was excited about the chance to take on fresh challenges and embark on new adventures that would allow me to continue my commitment to educating girls and women.

The first of the three opportunities came as a result of a discussion with Peter O'Neill, a friend from our early years as admissions directors. Peter had gone on to head Wooster School in Danbury, Connecticut, and then Garrison Forest School (GFS), an all-girls' boarding and day school outside Baltimore. He had also served as an NCGS board member and treasurer. Peter told me about a new venture at GFS made possible by an Edward E. Ford Foundation Leadership Challenge the school had received. The $250,000 matching grant was awarded to five independent schools to underwrite innovative, distinctive programs that could be nationally replicable. A GFS alumna and trustee, Amabel Boyce James '70, generously met the challenge, and the James Center was founded at GFS in 2008 with a mission of creating "Programs and Partnerships with a Public Purpose." Peter asked me to become the founding director of the Center, and I enthusiastically accepted. I felt so fortunate to be presented with such an exciting challenge at a time when I was ready for something new. Happily, I would be working with Andrea Perry, director of Special Programs at GFS. She had attended numerous NCGS events and conferences over the years, so we were well acquainted.

The James Center's motto was "Real World, Right Now," and students at GFS participated in an array of interwoven curricular and co-curricular programs in STEM, financial literacy, and leadership. "Schools, especially girls' schools, are educating girls not just to do, but to lead—to be rather than to seem," Peter wrote at the time of the Center's founding. "Our students need to think and act beyond our campus borders."

In order to provide opportunities for students beyond campus borders, we began to forge external partnerships between the Center and prominent organizations making a difference in the real world. Andrea developed an early partnership between the GFS STEM program (which became known as Women in Science and Engineering [WISE]) and Johns Hopkins University (JHU) in Baltimore. Students joined with university professors working at the School of Engineering, the Bloomberg School of Public Health, the Veterinary Science/Equine Science Program, and the Sheridan School of Library Science. Several days a week, they traveled to the JHU campus to participate in research and hands-on projects, giving them significant experience that often led to career choices they otherwise might have ignored. These GFS participants would bring their work back to school, giving presentations that highlighted the work they had done in concert with JHU professors. I particularly enjoyed these demonstrations, which harkened back to all the work we had done—and that was still being done—at NCGS.

Recognizing the importance of global perspectives, GFS students also competed each year for Jenkins Fellowships, which provided volunteer opportunities around the world. These fellowships had existed at the school since 1999, but they became one of the centerpieces of the James Center mission. Like the WISE participants, the five to six students who received fellowship grants for summer volunteer work made schoolwide presentations after their experience. One girl established a nonprofit to help children in Ghana, another helped clear bamboo in a rainforest, and a writing enthusiast published a book to support malaria prevention in Malawi.

In the early years of my time at the James Center, I devoted much of my energy to building a financial literacy program at Garrison Forest. I had never stopped believing in the importance of providing young women with the economic tools for living financially independent lives. I turned to my original mentor, Joline Godfrey from Independent Means, to help guide me and the school as we developed internal programming with a focus on the language and elements of good money sense. We sent several students to Camp $tart-Up, developed a series of seminars on money matters for seniors, held financial literacy workshops for parents, urged girls to keep spending diaries, created a philanthropy club, and urged faculty members to look within their existing lessons for places to insert discussions about how money related to the topics being covered.

As it turned out, another unexpected opportunity allowed my commitment to financial literacy for girls and women to head in a new direction. My second post-NCGS start-up experience was with a new nonprofit, the Baltimore Women's Giving Circle, for which I became a founding member. Although such philanthropic groups are now very popular, they were still young at the time, having sprung up in the late 1990s. Women around the country had begun to realize

that by pooling their philanthropic dollars they could make a bigger impact on nonprofit groups serving women and their families. Our group of 50 founding women wanted to create that impact in the greater Baltimore area. I felt honored to be involved with this "band of sisters" and loved the fact that we represented all kinds of communities across and around the city. Each founding member of the circle contributed $1,000, providing us a base fund of $50,000 to be distributed immediately. In the early days, I served on a committee that created marketing materials in an effort to recruit even more women. By 2023, our membership had grown to 450 women, and we awarded nearly $500,000 to a group of local nonprofits that year.

In an earlier chapter, I talked about the founding of new all-girls' public schools, in particular a set of Young Women's Leadership Schools that originated in New York City but soon branched out to other locales in Dallas, Chicago, and Philadelphia. A Baltimore go-getter named Brenda Brown Rever, a women's rights advocate and philanthropist, had heard about these initiatives and believed that our city needed to start a similar charter school. She knew of my work at NCGS and asked me to join with her and a handful of other Charm City women to launch such a venture—my third post-NCGS start-up. I had seen how successful the urban schools were in providing an education for inner-city girls, many with family members lacking high school diplomas. The objective of the Baltimore Leadership School for Young Women (BLSYW) was for each high school graduate to gain entrance to a college or trade school. A lottery-based admissions system offered this chance to motivated girls who wanted to improve their lot in life. Remembering that only two girls' public schools had existed in 1991, I jumped at the chance to help start another one.

Our first order of business involved finding an appropriate location to house the school. Fortunately, an abandoned mid-city YWCA building became available. Led by Brenda, I and the rest of the board worked to secure funding for both the purchase and the necessary renovations. The school opened in 2009 with 120 girls in grade 6, most of them African Americans from low-income families. Today BLSYW students from grades 6 through 12 enjoy small classes, personalized instruction, and college guidance aimed to equalize their chance of acceptance with peers graduating from private schools. Every graduating senior

January 2009 letter from Brenda Rever, president of the Baltimore Leadership School for Young Women (BLSYW), inviting Whitney Ransome to serve on the Board of Directors, which she accepted.

goes on to a place of further learning, including Baltimore City Community College, the University of Maryland, Johns Hopkins University, and a variety of trade schools. I've found over the years that attending a BLSYW graduation ceremony is an exciting and humbling experience.

With so much to do in the 10 years after leaving NCGS, I was not able to keep up an active awareness of the Coalition's activities, but I remained interested and informed. Susanne Beck became executive director after Meg Moulton's departure, serving from August 2009 to March 2011. Following her departure, Burch Ford, former NCGS board chair and retired head of Miss Porter's School, took the helm as president of the board, and Nancy Mugele, currently head of Kent School in Chestertown, Maryland, served as interim executive director from July 2011 through July 2012. After an extensive search, Megan Murphy, former director of development at Marlborough School in Los Angeles, became executive director. She continues to do an outstanding job advancing the organization's goals, helping grow the membership, and expanding its scope to become the International Coalition of Girls' Schools (ICGS) in 2022.

    Megan has retained the tradition of working virtually and remotely. The current ICGS team includes eight full-time-equivalent staff members located in North America, Australia, and England. Often new leaders move forward with a strategic agenda and don't look back. This is not Megan's way. She frequently reached out to Meg and me by acknowledging and celebrating the early foundational work we had done. We received invitations for the 20th and 25th anniversaries of NCGS, were asked to offer our thoughts on the formative years, and were graciously recognized whenever we attended the June Annual Meeting. I was happy to maintain such a warm connection, because I knew how much the skills and experience I had gained at NCGS helped guide my later work and keep me rooted in my lifelong commitment to girls, their education, and their futures.

–XVIII–
Parting Words

*Don't look at your feet to see if you are doing it right.
Just dance.*

— ANNE LAMOTT, *BIRD BY BIRD*

When I think about my life so far, I'm reminded of the work of Dr. Mary Catherine Bateson, the daughter of Margaret Mead and a graduate of Brearley, an all girls' school in New York City. In her 1991 book, *Composing a Life*, Bateson suggests that we often look at our experiences in hindsight and find patterns much like in a finished quilt. She mentions the creative potential of complex lives, where energies are not narrowly focused on a single ambition but rather attuned to the benefits of redefining goals as our ambitions evolve. Bateson concludes that life is an improvisational art form that features interruptions, conflicted priorities, and unexpected challenges. Rather than viewing these outside forces as impeding our ambitions, we should embrace them as meaningful pieces of a richly patterned life.

Writing this book has shown me the truth in Bateson's words. By telling this story, I've come to see threads in my life that connect in ways I hadn't previously noticed. I realize now that what once seemed like separate occurrences or unwelcome interruptions actually helped shape the strong beliefs that have become my life's passion. Believing in the power and significance of girls' education is the North Star of my life and career. While there was no road map for what we were doing, our path forward involved adventure, surprises, hard work, and great rewards. It was a privilege and an honor to have helped make a difference in the resurgence of girls' schools, and I hope this story encourages others to continue the work we have begun.

Above: The family at Kate's college graduation in 2008.

Right: Tom, Whitty, Kate, and Christopher in 1992 while at Concord Academy.

APPENDIX A

The Evolution of the NCGS Merger

JUNE 1989

- Meg Moulton presents final Ransome/Maguire research report to Coalition of Girls' Boarding School (CGBS) members at special meeting at Emma Willard School
- Arlene Gibson, Kent Place School, sends letter to day school heads to suggest a meeting in November at Headmistresses of the East Conference

SEPTEMBER 1989

- CGBS hires Ransome and Moulton to serve as executive directors to carry out research report recommendations

OCTOBER 1989

- CGBS Directory of 31 schools is produced. Rachel Belash/Olive Long appointed co-chairs of CGBS

NOVEMBER 1989

- Coalition of Girls' Day Schools (CGDS) Steering Committee formed at Headmistresses meeting in Princeton. Arlene Gibson is chair and asks each school to send $500 to pay for an alumnae research project.

FEBRUARY 1990

- CGDS hires Yankleovich, Shulman and Clancy and Howard Rubenstein Associates as research and public relations consultants

MAY 1990

- 30 days schools belong to CGDS (some with boarding divisions). Goal is to get 50 schools into membership to fund the alumnae research and PR project. Cost will be $6,000 per school.

JUNE 1990

- Boarding schools' participation in the CGDS projects is sought at the June CGBS meeting

SEPTEMBER 1990
- CGDS publicizes the results of alumnae survey of over 1,200 girls' school graduates.
- Positive press coverage ensues.

JUNE 1991
- CGBS has second annual meeting at Foxcroft School June 23-24 with 48 participants (16 heads and 32 admissions professionals attend).
- Steering Committee led by Co-Chairs Mary Lou Leipheimer and Olive Long recommends merger with CGDS.
- Membership votes to approve the measure.

JULY 1991
- Arlene Gibson writes CGDS members informing them of CGBS's interest in a merger.
- Steering Committees of CGDS and CGBS meet on July 2 and agree to a merger.

SEPTEMBER 1991
- CGBS co-chairs write to members about the benefits of a merger. Steering committee of CGDS writes its members offering the same information

OCTOBER 1991
- CGBS and CGDS leadership, along with Emily Grotta and Wendy Schwimmer of Rubenstein Associates, meet in NYC and develop a working outline of a merged administration and division of responsibilities.

NOVEMBER 1991
- CGBS and CGDS Steering Committees meet at Headmistresses of the East Conference in New Jersey.
- They agree to form the National Coalition of Girls Schools (NCGS).
- Mary Lou Leipheimer, Olive Long, and Arlene Gibson serve as co-chairs of the new Steering Committee.
- Whitney Ransome and Meg Moulton remain as co-executive directors
- Howard Rubenstein Associates is rehired as public relations counsel.
- 56 schools are in the merged membership.
- Whitney and Meg present a detailed organizational outline.

JANUARY 1992
- *Education Week* reports the mergers and NCGS gets announced and publicized in a wide variety of ways.

APPENDIX B

"Role of the Coalition" *

Introduction

Previous sections of this report are replete with research findings and strategic initiatives that are relevant to the future direction and objectives of the Coalition. The value and benefits of collective action need not be repeated in great detail. Suffice it to say that, armed with current research, the Coalition is poised to pursue a larger share of the independent school market. Collective action not only offers individual schools heightened status and visibility but also the potential for alternative uses of school personnel and financial resources due to savings achieved through Coalition endeavors on behalf of the membership.

One of the first assignments for the Steering Committee is the setting of priorities and the development of an Action Plan. Much of what follows is directed at achieving these priorities.

Organizational Mission and Focus

The Coalition has quickly evolved from the brainchild of one to the cause of many. The coming together of heads and directors of admission for the common good of girls' boarding schools was no small achievement. Coupled with the commitment to and funding of market research, the group is now ready to broaden its organizational horizons. The Steering Committee should continue to be the operative force behind an expanded role for the Coalition. The suggestions listed below can serve as the core of meeting agendas over the next year.

- Develop a one page mission statement for the Coalition.
- Establish short- and long- term goals for achieving these objectives.
- Make professional development and advice for member schools an auxiliary goal of the Coalition.
- Define the qualifications for Coalition membership and what is expected from member institutions.
- Consider offering special status to girls' day schools.

Administrative Structuring

The recommendations in this report will have no impact if there is no one with the time, energy, talent, or resources to implement them. The Steering Committee deserves credit for taking the Coalition through the initial phases of the development. Such a committee should continue to exist, aided by the full-time help of a paid professional who reports directly to this group.

- Appoint an Executive Director of the Coalition.
- Seek office space and staff support from a member school or affinity organization.
- Establish a yearly budget tying it to annual action plans.
- Seek liaisons with existing organizations already serving most member schools.
- Discuss the ongoing role and responsibilities of the Steering Committee and determine nominating procedures for rotation of current members.

Funding and Support

The Coalition has been fortunate to have had special funding for market research from both member schools and foundations. This willingness and interest in financing special projects for the cause of girls' boarding education is an encouraging sign. Armed with the findings and suggestions from the Ransome/Maguire and EMC project, the Coalition should make as one of its top priorities the securing of additional funding as it moves into another level of organization and development. While external funding is obviously desirable, the future of the Coalition should not rest on it. Schools must be prepared to support these joint endeavors.

- Establish a viable and equitable dues structure for member schools.
- Highlight for members services rendered for dues and develop a rationale for belonging that makes joining the coalition the "thing to do."
- Seek "start-up" funding from foundations and organizations that are attuned or could become attuned to the value of all-girls' education.
- Review yearly projects and plans as they may relate to a particular foundation's interest in funding a one-time only undertaking.
- Discuss whether carefully chosen alumnae from member schools may be approached for special donations to the cause of women's education in general through the work of the Coalition.

Tasks for the Coalition

Much awaits the executive director in the way of program possibilities once the preceding steps have been accomplished. The list below suggests some of the general tasks for consideration.

- Public Relations Agent
- Communications Center
- Clearing House for Information and Research
- Research Sponsor
- National Talent Searcher
- Professional Development Provider

Conclusion

Market research has offered the Coalition a myriad of possibilities. The challenge for the Steering Committee is how to put good ideas to work in an effective and meaningful way. Perceptions in the marketplace suggest there are families interested and willing to make the commitment to girls' boarding education. The Coalition and its members have much to do to show these potential constituents how and why their daughters should be tomorrow's alumnae.

---

*The complete chapter, written by Whitney Ransome, appeared as the final piece of the initial market research project conducted by Enrollment Management Consultants and Ransome/Maguire and commissioned by the National Coalition of Girls' Schools.

APPENDIX C

Ransome Prize Winners

Alice Phillips *2023 – 2024*

Martha Perry *2022 – 2023*

Jeanne Goka *2021 – 2022*

Patricia Hayot* *2019 – 2020*

Betty White *2018 – 2019*

Trudy Hall *2017 – 2018*

Ann Teaff *2016 – 2017*

Concepcion R. Alvar *2015 – 2016*

Ann Pollina *2014 – 2015*

Margaret R. Broad *2013 – 2014*

Rosalyn Wood and Susan Casey *2011 – 2012*

Susan R. Groesbeck *2010 – 2011*

Springside School student group *2009 – 2010*

Jane O'Connor *2008 – 2009*

*Honored at the 2021 NCGS Virtual Conference

APPENDIX D

THE WHITE HOUSE
WASHINGTON

September 20, 2000

WARM GREETING TO EVERYONE gathered in Boston for the National Conference on Girls, Women and Money, sponsored by the National Coalition of Girls' Schools.

Women and girls must never believe that there are limitations on what they can do or become in this country. That is why all of us have a responsibility to renew our commitment to gender equality in every aspect of society.

This innovative national conference reinforces that commitment by bringing together educators, business professionals, psychologists, entrepreneurs, financial experts, and other leaders to focus on the unique challenges women face in the marketplace and to share effective programs and policies to assist women in achieving financial independence.

I commend the organizers and participants of this event for promoting financial empowerment and economic literacy for women and girls. By contributing to their professional, educational, and economic advancement, you are helping a new generation of leaders to make their own important contributions to the life of our nation and the strength of our economy.

Hillary joins me in extending best wishes for a productive conference and every success its your efforts.

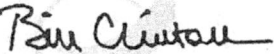

ACKNOWLEDGMENTS

I have a long list of people who have influenced my life, set me on a path of writing, and supported my effort to tell my story. No list can capture all who have made a difference. I am deeply grateful to those mentioned below and to the many others whose names are not here.

Frank Brogan served as my first mentor, urging me to attend the Key West Literary Seminar in 2000 when the theme was memoir writing. He also gave me my first Admissions job in Florida back in 1974.

In Key West I met Margaret Thomas in a writing workshop. A published author from my home state of New Jersey, Poochy became a fast friend, and we exchanged writing drafts.

Madeline Blais led that workshop in Key West and got me believing that I could write.

Another year at the Key West workshop, I participated in author Mary Morris's workshop and felt encouraged by her as well.

When I settled in Baltimore, I attended a memoir course at Johns Hopkins University headed by Margaret Osburn, another writer who became my guide in her weekly sessions at her home. Early on, she encouraged me to write this book.

Rachel Belash, Arlene Gibson, Mary Lou Leipheimer, and Olive Long had the vision and hutzpah needed to reverse the downward slide of girls' school enrollments. There are dozens of others, including an array of outstanding NCGS Board Chairs and trustees who redefined why girls' schools matter.

Meg Moulton, my partner of close to 20 years: I couldn't have accomplished half of what I did without her by my side. NCGS would never have prospered without our teamwork, determination, sense of humor, complementary talents, and fearless belief that what we were doing mattered. We were nimble, entrepreneurial, and ready to tackle any obstacle. By a host of measures, we succeeded.

Carol Mann Sacknoff gave dozens of years of invaluable work to Concord Academy. One of her unofficial but critical tasks involved her undying friendship, love, and loyalty to me during my 19 years at the school. The life of a head of school spouse has its rewards and challenges. Carol understood both. In addition to helping with the most challenging part of the work, she and I were "Queens of Frou Frous" at countless CA events. We took great pleasure in taking entertaining to new heights. I wouldn't have survived without her.

Sue Sauer and Ann Parke ran the NCGS office (and sometimes me!) and kept the operation on track and in good order. During their respective times as administrative directors, they fueled our work in quiet yet efficient ways.

Sara White Lennon was the NCGS publications designer for close to 17 years. Her artistic talents and creative designs made everything we produced in print and online stand out.

Caroline Colletti served as our very able director of communications at NCGS and frequent writer and designer of our publications.

My sister, Susie Ransome, was a great support in this writing project, helping me with many of the organizational tasks.

Megan Murphy, executive director of the International Coalition of Girls' Schools (formerly NCGS), and Paige Rannigan, director of finance and operations, were remarkably helpful. They provided sustained support by sharing valuable archival materials, offering encouragement, and consistently expressing their belief in the project. I couldn't have done it without them.

Lucille Stott, my coach, editor, and companion on this project believed in the value of my work and in 2015 urged me to write about it. I wasn't ready at that time, but she kept the faith, and when I turned to her this year she said, "Let's do it."

My early readers, Tom Wilcox, Rachel Belash, Arlene Gibson, Peter O'Neill, and Megan Murphy, gave their time and valuable perspectives to the manuscript and helped make this a better book.

The talented and generous Deborah Gray scoured the manuscript with her keen eye for language and usage and gave it a welcome polish.

My good friend, Dr. Ann Macaulay, offered great encouragement and support. In addition to her belief in the project, she photographed me as I sorted archival files last summer. The view of my summer desk was her idea.

Designer *extraordinaire*—and also a Concord Academy alumna and trustee— Irene Chu has been an invaluable partner in making this book come alive.

I would never have succeeded in completing this project without the love, support, and patience of my family. Tom Wilcox, my husband of almost 45 years, never stopped believing in me and what I might accomplish. He tolerated my home office, stood with me during tough moments, improved my writing through his loving review of my work, celebrated my successes, and never challenged how I led my life, both professionally and personally. Always a partner!

And to my two children, Katherine Ransome Wilcox and Christopher Ransome Wilcox, thank you for putting up with an often distracted working Mom who loves you unconditionally.

Whitty's desk in her Canada studio, where she wrote the first three chapters of *Why Girls' Schools Matter*.

ABOUT THE AUTHOR

Whitney "Whitty" Ransome grew up in southern New Jersey and graduated from Moorestown Friends School. She earned a BA in Political Science from the University of North Carolina at Greensboro and an MA in American Studies from the University of Miami. Before co-founding the National Coalition of Girls' Schools (NCGS) with her co-executive director Meg Moulton, she was a classroom teacher and a director of admissions and financial aid. Long an advocate of women's rights, she was the Equal Rights Amendment coordinator for Common Cause in Florida in the 1970s. During her 20-year career with the NCGS, she helped promote the benefits of single-sex education for girls throughout the United States and beyond. Since leaving NCGS in 2008, she has served as the founding director of the James Center at Garrison Forest School, an all girls' school outside Baltimore; a founding member of the Baltimore Women's Giving Circle; and a board member of several nonprofits, including the Baltimore Leadership School for Young Women. She currently lives in Florida and Canada with her husband, Thomas E. Wilcox.

Author Photo by H Wetzel

www.ingramcontent.com/pod-product-compliance
Lightning Source LLC
Chambersburg PA
CBHW081430070526
44586CB00020B/2545